Bibl
in b

Diether Lauenstein

Biblical rhythms
in biography

Floris Books

Translated by James H. Hindes

First published in German under the title
Der Lebenslauf und seine Gesetze
by Verlag Urachhaus, Stuttgart, 1974
First published in English in 1983 by Floris Books

British Library Cataloguing in Publication Data

Lauenstein, Diether
    Biblical rhythms in biography.
    1. Biography
    I. Title   II. Hindes, James H.
    III. Der Lebenslauf und seine Gesetze. *English*
    920'.001   CT31

ISBN 0-86315-001-2

Printed in Great Britain
at the University Press, Oxford

Contents

3 The Gifts of the Hierarchies

Translator's Foreword

In autumn of 1972, Dr Diether Lauenstein gave three lectures in Stuttgart, Germany, on the laws of human biography. His topic, though not unknown, was not yet the focus of widespread public attention it is today. By now, the idea that there are predictable crises of adult life has been brought to the attention of millions. Back in 1972, however, it was still in the process of being discovered and clearly formulated by sociologists, psychologists and other professionals around the world. In America, in 1973, researchers at Harvard, the University of Chicago, and the University of California at Berkeley and Los Angeles were independently studying events and crises typical of all biographies. Clearly, here was a case of simultaneity at work; an idea had come of age.

Mankind, at least western man, had discovered that the human being has not only a physical shape or form, which can be objectively studied, but that furthermore he has a profile or shape in time whose curves and characteristics can likewise be investigated. Unfortunately, there is no single word in the English language that adequately captures this newly-discovered entity. For this reason, in some passages I have decided to retain the German word *Zeitgestalt* used by Dr Lauenstein in the original text. Both parts of this word have already found some currency in the English language. 'Gestalt', according to *Webster's Third New International Dictionary,* means: 'a structure or configuration of physical, biological, or psychological phenomena so integrated as to constitute a functional unit with properties not derivable from its parts in summation.' The emphasis here is on *wholeness*. Since the word *Zeitgeist*, meaning 'spirit of an age' or 'spirit of the times', is not unknown in English, it was felt that the word *Zeitgestalt* would be understandable as 'a shape in time, showing wholeness'.

To my knowledge, this is the first study of biography appearing in English to explore the religious dimension of man's profile in time. Precisely this religious element is reflected in the emphasis on wholeness found in the word *Zeitgestalt*. The wholeness to be found in every biography is usually greater than the wholeness we feel in our souls; for this reason our *Zeitgestalt* is given to us by God to lead us to greater integration and wholeness of personality. The religious perspective seeks, then, to find within each individual destiny itself at least a reflection, however much distorted, of the wholeness of God. Today, the faith that our *Zeitgestalt* has originated in the world of the divine and is working to balance, harmonize and complete our fragmented selves has a special significance. Such faith forms the necessary starting point for a conscious cooperation with the angelic world in creating destiny. This cooperation is, of course, as difficult as it is necessary and, as modern human beings, we seek some justification of our faith. Herein lies the uniqueness of Dr Lauenstein's contribution: he uses his vast knowledge of the Bible, world history, theology and philosophy, plus his own considerable life experience, to show (admittedly in an arduously condensed form) the origin of the *Zeitgestalt*, its evolution and man's awareness thereof, from early biblical times to the present.

The first chapter derives its method and content from the account of creation found in Genesis, while the third is built upon and develops St Paul's teachings concerning the angelic hierarchies. The second chapter presents observations and conclusions based directly upon life experience and can therefore be read first, or even by itself.

A word concerning the translation itself: Dr Lauenstein's prose is as terse as it is profound. For this reason, I have sometimes taken the liberty of rendering his thoughts into English rather than translating exact words or sentences. Before the translation was begun, he gave his approval to this approach, and with his trust, I have striven throughout to remain true to his thoughts and intentions.

James H. Hindes

Acknowledgment

Unless otherwise stated, all quotations from the Bible are from the Revised Standard Version with kind permission of the National Council of Churches of Christ. (New Testament © 1946, 1971; Old Testament © 1952.) Italics in the quotations are the author's.

1 The Measure of Creation

1.1 *The* Zeitgestalt

The human being lives in space and time. He lives in space with his body and in time most consciously through memories, either personal, biographical or historical. The form of the human body, its shape and contours in space, can be studied through art. Every body, though unique, shares certain elements with all others. More than this all bodies possess characteristics in common with the very archetype of the human form. No other people studied the human form with as much devotion as the ancient Greeks. Through their sculpture, they approached an understanding of the archetype of the human body. And while the Greeks were so deeply engaged in this study of man's shape in space, another Mediterranean culture strove simultaneously to understand his shape or profile in time, his *Zeitgestalt*. That was ancient Israel, whose holy scripture is preserved for us in the Old Testament. The Israelites were the first people to understand themselves as a nation with a national history. Ironically enough this was only finally achieved in the sixth century BC when, during the Babylonian captivity, to all outward appearances Jewish history had come to a tragic end.

1.2 *Early Biographies*

A brief sketch of the earliest stages in the development of a biographical consciousness begins with the Greeks. Originally the Greeks looked at only two specific ages in life which represented two important high points: around the twentieth year when the physical body was perfected and the fortieth when, as they assumed, the life of the soul, that is the personality, had developed itself fully. But the developing or 'unfolding' of the personality they did not examine. The development of the individual in general and the significance of the decline of life in particular were not studied. It was Plato who first noted that man's spirit only really begins to awaken as the body grows weak and fades with age. He was the first to see so clearly that Socrates' life and teaching form a unity, that his life and actions, his suffering and death constitute a clearer and deeper statement than any merely verbal explanation. The description in the *Meno* of Socrates' last days speaks eloquently of this insight into the unity of word and deed. Although Plato did not describe the death of his master with the same awareness for the changing qualitative value of each hour that we find in the four Gospels' descriptions of the end of Jesus' life — still he is very exact. In reading the lives of Jesus and Socrates, our consciousness of time in hours is focused around the court proceedings and the death that was in each case outwardly violent yet inwardly so triumphant. Plato's only other efforts in this field are found in the seventh of his *Letters*. Written and sent to a friend in Syracuse in 345 BC when Plato was seventy-three years old, it includes an auto-biographical sketch which, because the purpose of the letter lay elsewhere, was unfortunately very incomplete.

In China one hundred years before Christ the great historian Ssŭ-ma Ch'ien, a court astrologer by profession, wrote biographies of Chinese statesmen. His intention in writing, however, never rose above the level of moral admonishment. Two hundred years later

Plutarch, in describing the lives of eminent Greeks and Romans, was also to remain at this stage of biography.

In India the life of Gautama Buddha was conscientiously written down by his followers in the sixth century BC. With the exception of his death this life appears on the surface very similar to that of Jesus. Yet it was viewed by Buddha himself and his disciples not as a historical, unrepeatable event as we understand the life of Jesus, but as a particularly fortunate example of a pattern according to which the life of every perfected or spiritually fully-awakened human being should unfold. According to this view it is, however, not necessary for every follower of Buddha to first become a prince, as Gautama was. Neither must everyone do as he did and first acquire a son, whom he later called a 'fetter'. Still, other Buddhas are always portrayed passing through the same spiritually important stations occurring in the master's life and regularly experiencing the same things. The writers of these Buddha biographies were not seeking the individuality of the Buddha himself but rather the archetype of 'Buddhahood' existing far above it. The variety of earthly Buddhas arises from the different historical situations in which they lived; and the great variety of human lives, when compared with this archetypical Buddha, are seen in Buddhistic terms either as a humanity not yet fully achieved or yet again gone astray. For Buddhists there is only one path to the spirit and therefore only one possible biography that stands the spiritual test. Biography as a description of individual life histories would, for Buddhists, merely be a recounting of the endless variations of human error, not worth recording.

During the last centuries before Christ's appearance, efforts were made throughout the civilized world to

13

understand not only history but also the shape of an individual human being's biography in time, his *Zeitgestalt*. The greatest success in this endeavour was achieved by the authors of the four Gospels in their descriptions of the life of Jesus, particularly in their accounts of his suffering and death. I say this knowing full well the claims of modern biblical criticism. Reaching a high point with Bultmann this criticism asserts that we only know with complete certainty a few phrases spoken by Jesus. But the Gospels do give us a great deal of accurate information concerning Jesus' last days and hours. And we learn at least something of biographical value concerning the other years of his ministry. His youth and birth, however, appear only on the periphery; they also present us with the most riddles. The apostle Paul is also thinking of the individual human being when he declares the differences among people to be God-intended; and counts all men as members of the body of Christ, each having his own special abilities and unique task (1Cor.12:12).

Ancient Israel's efforts to understand how the course of time influences the evolution of the individual human being have been taken up and brought to completion by Christianity. This advance was made possible when the course of every individual life and not only that of the Master, the founder of Christianity, was seen as a means of revelation, as a vehicle through which a spiritual entity evolves visibly in time. Yet Christians still needed centuries to grasp fully this new insight.

It was the church father Augustine who discovered a basic law in his life existing above the Mosaic moralizing plane, a level on which he indulges himself more than most modern readers are comfortable with. This law was, however, not to be found in his successes; as a new purely spiritual principle it could be seen most readily, oddly enough, shining through the declining half of his life rather than in the dazzling rise to prominence which marked the first part of his career. The same discovery had already been made by the prophet Elijah (1Kings 19:15–18) twelve hundred years earlier in the destiny of the people of Israel. This naturally heart-breaking discovery was later raised to full consciousness in the writings of the prophets, above all in those of Jeremiah. The 'great divide' in Augustine's life occurred in his thirty-third year. Something entirely new became visible in his life at that time which he tentatively labelled 'predestination': an incomparable spiritual brilliance that continued to shine over the descending half of his life. Only through such careful observations do the events occurring in an individual's life fall into a coherent structure in time; all genuine biography reveals such a structure. All of this is described by Augustine in his *Confessions*.

Almost immediately after Augustine had discovered man's precise *Zeitgestalt* or 'biographical contours', the culture of late antiquity, now become Christian, began to hide man's spatial shape, his physical body. From the sixth century onward in the new capital of antiquity, Byzantium, even the athletes in the circus appeared in high-collared full attire. The Christian world's turnabout with respect to Greek antiquity was based on preliminary work accomplished by Israel. Therefore it is natural for us initially to look in the Bible for the basic laws of biography, of the *Zeitgestalt,* man's 'shape in time'. In any case, from beginning to end, the Bible contains stories of human destinies, although the perspective is, at first, more that of mankind and of certain peoples. For the purposes of our enquiry we are not

15

concerned whether or not contemporary historians would consider the events recorded in the Bible as central, if they would employ biblical mythology or any myths at all, in their efforts to understand primordial history. We seek here not historical facts as such but rather concepts and ideas most helpful for an understanding of those facts. Such conceptual tools are always best taken from those who first recognized them, a principle which holds for all disciplines. In this case it was the wise men of Israel who first prepared the way.

This chapter will, therefore, be devoted to the Bible. In the second chapter we shall describe general characteristics of human biography observable without reference to the Bible. But because the basic principle we shall develop from Genesis can save us time we shall use it as a guide for what follows. In the third chapter we shall be concerned with the role played by the angels in human lives; at least, to the extent that this influence can be observed. Then, with this second guiding principle we shall be able to survey briefly, yet thoroughly, the spiritual life of the individual and of mankind.

1.3 The individual and humanity

Every part of the Bible is filled almost exclusively with stories and events taken from human life. However, from the beginning to the end of the Old Testament the levels on which these stories are told constantly change. The same thing happens in the New Testament from the four Gospels to the Book of Revelation, in reverse correspondence with the levels in the Old Testament. The Bible at the beginning speaks of the first couple, Adam and Eve, then of the primordial fathers up to the dispersion of the nations with the Tower of Babel. Thus far it is concerned with the development of humanity in general. Then, from Abraham to the prophet Malachi or the Maccabees the focus is on the people of Israel. Any individuals appearing in either of these two great parts of the Old Testament represent not themselves but rather a nation of people or all mankind. The lives of David and several of the kings of Judah also contain this universal characteristic, representing as they do, all mankind. We shall have much more to say about David's life in the second chapter. But certain universal laws applying to the life of any individual can already be read at this stage from the life of Adam, who represents primordial man. These three levels, mankind, folk and individual human being can be compared with one another for they all reflect the same eternal laws of development. The facts of the life of David assure us of this; the Gospels express the same view when they place details from the life of Jesus alongside details from the history of Israel; even Paul compares Jesus with Adam (1Cor.15:45).

The Gospels tell us the life of a single individual: Jesus of Nazareth. They relate his life to the history of his people and mankind. Yet it no longer appears embedded in the greater framework of contemporary history as do the stories of the Patriarchs, Moses and David. Only in brief mention in the background do nation and the rest of humanity become visible in the Gospels. Because of this restraint the writers are all the more able to make the archetype of every destiny recognizable in an immediate fashion through the life and death of Jesus.

The Acts of the Apostles follow the Gospels in the New Testament. The deeds of various individuals in the service of Christ are described, particularly those of

Paul. In his life we see a strange interweaving of two different kinds of scenes: firstly, those which could almost be taken from the life of Jesus, for example his court trial in Jerusalem; and secondly, a totally different kind of scene revealing guilt, such as his initial persecution of the Christians or a much later one when he took an oath in the Temple according to Jewish ritual — at James's insistence — in order to display his faithfulness to Moses, a faithfulness that no longer existed. That appearance in the Temple sent him directly to trial before a Roman procurator. This life and death situation for Paul followed a course similar to that of Jesus' trial. The law which Augustine discovered 350 years later could actually have been deciphered from this two-fold interweaving of threads in Paul's life: the one personal, the other received from Christ.

The next stage in the New Testament is reflected by the letters of the Apostles to the new Christian communities, which are to take the place formerly occupied by a nation united through blood. The conclusion is then formed by the Apocalypse, which describes in awesome pictures the future course of humanity until the end of the earth and its renewal. We can see here a uniform bow extending through the entire Bible: beginning with Adam representing mankind, descending to the level of a nation, that is a community of people united through blood ties, to the individual life of Jesus Christ; upwards again to the deeds of individuals in the service of Christ, and back then to the community and to a new mankind.

1.4 The law of beginnings

In this chapter we shall be chiefly occupied with mankind's beginning. Beginnings are always important because no man, no community, and altogether no organic whole can ever escape the laws inaugurated at the inception of a new order. For this reason we must assume that Adam's deeds and sufferings contain the laws of development, not only for mankind as a whole, but also for the life of every human being. In the New Testament the Gospels simply assume that Jesus' life can be used as a standard of comparison and Paul even compares Adam with Jesus, calling him a *túpos*, a particular kind of 'prototype' (Rom.5:14). We shall see later where this assumption leads us. Finally, the life of David, who as king also represented his people, will serve as a connecting link between these three levels on which destiny unfolds (humanity, nation, individual).

1.5 Regular and irregular events in life

In every human life there are two clearly distinguishable streams, one regular and the other irregular. The first stream consists of events and rhythms that can be portrayed in numbers and laws. The irregular stream moves back and forth between guilt and atonement, sin and forgiveness. Church tradition and biblical interpretation have invariably focused their attention on this latter, more obviously moral, stream while neglecting or even completely forgetting the former. Yet only the laws and forces woven into life in a regular fashion make a thorough understanding of biography possible. Irregular factors usually explain only details. Here we shall listen also to what the Bible has to say concerning the

regular laws of biography. This may be unusual for
biblical exegesis, but we achieve thereby the groundwork upon which a truly Christian teaching of sin and
forgiveness is based. We learn to view sin and guilt not
as the sad shadow-substance of which human lives, until
atonement, are constituted. That is Buddhism. We find
rather that the regularities in life provide the basis for
individual conversion, atonement, enhancement of the
spiritual person and real achievement in life. The
rhythms of life also make possible the Christian virtues
of spiritual devotion and faith which, when developed
in freedom, pave the way for the development of a
strong, free individual personality.

1.6 David's life

David's life (1042–972 BC) as we find in the Old Testament books of Samuel and the Kings was filled with
references to the origins of his people and the beginnings
of mankind. Without knowing it, his objective in life
was to live out the basic laws of human destiny inaugurated at the beginning. In his life, history is reflected
all the way back to the very beginning.

David is first mentioned in the Bible in connection
with a sacrifice near Bethlehem which the prophet and
judge Samuel performed for David's family. Samuel
drew the twelve-year-old David into the ceremony. This
premature involvement in the religious world of adults
resulted in David's confirmation as well as his secret
anointing to be the future king (1Sam.16). In his encounter with Goliath at seventeen we find the event that
became symbolic for his life altogether. The Bible points
to this when once again reminding us of Goliath just
before David's death (2Sam.21:19).

After the encounter with Goliath, the course of David's life traces in reverse order the steps of Israel's and mankind's development. Until David, Israel's wandering had not yet ended, had not yet fully taken root in the land of Canaan. We read that this finally occurred through David's conquering Jerusalem and then transplanting the ark of the Covenant to that location (2Sam.7:10).

When David fled from Saul, his wandering parallels Israel's forty years in the desert. He protected the farmers of Judea and the Philistines from the Amalek, the fierce tribe of desert robbers. For this reason the farmers supplied him and his troops with food. Just as the people of Israel had fought in the past, so he fought now with the cry: 'A hand upon the banner of the LORD! The LORD will have war with Amalek from generation to generation.' (Exod.17:16.)

When he was crowned king over all Judea in Hebron, we hear the words of the Lord, 'You are my son, today I have begotten you.' (Ps.2:7.) As God's spokesman, Moses had already confessed to the pharaoh concerning the people of Israel, 'Israel is my first-born son' (Exod.4:22). And when seven years after his coronation David sat on the throne of Melchizedek in Jerusalem his path had taken him, as it were, back to Abraham, who had been blessed in Jerusalem by the priest-king Melchizedek himself (Ps.110:4; Gen.14:17–20).

David's adultery with Bathsheba was to follow later in Jerusalem. Here his sin was like a repetition of the ancient error of mankind before the Flood, when 'the sons of God saw that the daughters of men were fair; and they took to wife such of them as they chose . . . and they bore children to them. These were the mighty men that were of old . . .' (Gen.6:2,4).

Next in David's life came the murder of one son by another and Absalom's insurrection, forcing David from his city, the 'city of David'. The archetypes for these acts are provided by Cain and Abel, and Adam's expulsion from the Garden of Eden (Gen.3–4).

The Scriptures describe the beginning of the world as a creation in six days and God's last work was the creation of man. He created the spiritual seed for man with the words: 'Let us make man in our image, after our likeness' (Gen.1:26). With another sin, his last, David reached all the way back to the stage of creation marked by these words. He ordered that all able-bodied men capable of bearing arms be counted. The old king had lived a rich and, as we have seen, a divinely ordered life. Still he did not yet understand the basic law of mankind: the fact that the image of God is to be found in every human being and not merely in special individuals who may be so brilliant as to be called 'sons of God'.

Through the plague sent as punishment for the first census, David finally understood this fact. Then, for reconciliation with God he sought and found the proper location for the Temple, the threshing floor of Araunah, north of the city. Here Solomon was later actually to build the Temple.

The purchase of a plot of ground for the Temple was, in fact, the only suitable expiation for this particular sin. For the Solomonic Temple, through its arrangement and proportions and through the sacred services held within it, which acted to mediate the eternal into space and time, ensured that the image of God would live in the midst of the people and ultimately in the people themselves. It preserved the people from the ruin of the Great Number, from falling to the level of the depersonalized numbered masses, in which the Israelites necessarily had to live from that time on as both citizens and soldiers of a great nation. We today also live in such a society. From then on only in the service of the Temple did the people of God remain divided into twelve tribes as the twelve constellations in the sky. The promise to Abraham that his descendants would be 'as the stars of heaven and as the sand which is on the seashore' (Gen.22:17) had been fulfilled. When the great king died at the age of seventy, his life had followed a path going back to the spiritual creation of man, to the time when God said, 'Let us make man in our image, after our likeness' (Gen.1:26). The very thing which the census would negate becomes visible through David's expiation.

1.7 Ten sayings of God concerning man

The deepest secrets of mankind's becoming are hidden in David's biography. In Adam however, the man of the beginning, we find the human being portrayed more clearly than in any later figure in the Bible. We would expect then, to find the *Zeitgestalt*, the profile of man's biography in time, most clearly expressed there. And we find just such an expression in Genesis, chapters one to three, when God speaks to, or concerning, man on ten separate occasions. The words then spoken are called sayings of God.

Before we continue with these ten sayings let us reconsider the significance of death in biography. The expectation of death combined with a life-span whose length can easily be surveyed provides man with the foundation for a biographical consciousness. Higher animals live entirely in the momentary experience and cannot, therefore, develop an individual profile in time and certainly no biography. One could, of course, construct a history of the events occurring in an animal's life. However, such a history would have no 'inside': that is, it could not be experienced by the animal itself as a meaningful sequence. The Bible first hints at this hidden element of death in human biography in the story of Noah's ark when the Lord says before the Flood, 'My spirit shall not abide in man for ever, for he is flesh, but his days shall be a hundred and twenty years' (Gen.6:3). As we saw, the biographies of Socrates and Jesus also 'crystallized', as it were, around their death. The meaning of their lives condenses at this time; every hour has its own special quality.

If death makes the shape of life possible then it is from birth that life's substance flows. And, as one might suspect, many of the events occurring in life that are regular and predictable flow from this pole of life. We can begin to understand these forces from birth and their impact on biography by seeing them in the mirror of the creation account of the Bible, specifically, in the ten sayings, the words spoken by the Godhead concerning man.

In the two accounts of creation (Gen.1–3), in the primordial history from Cain to Noah (Gen.4–9), and also in the account of the origins of nations and languages up to the covenant God made with Abraham (Gen.10–22) — in each of these first three sections of the Bible God speaks either to man, or concerning him, ten times. These three sections can be recognized in the text through the repetition of important sentences. The first series of these sayings of God begins with the unusual plural: 'Let *us* . . .' (Gen.1:26) and then repeats it at the end, 'Adam has become as one of *us*' (Gen.3:22) and then again at the beginning of the third series: 'Come, let *us* go down, and there confuse their language' (Gen.11:7). Nowhere else in the Bible does the Godhead speak this way in the plural. For brevity we shall concern ourselves here only with the first series of divine sayings, occasionally quoting from the second and third series for the sake of comparison.

1. With God's first words concerning man, 'Let us make man in our image, after our likeness' (Gen.1:26), the Bible signifies the fundamental law of man's spiritual being and earthly existence. Creation has been for man's sake. He is its goal and simultaneously the image of God. That means an individual human being is worth more than the entire physical world, a fact first expressed by St Teresa of Avila. This idea with its enormous implications is also to be found in the *Gospel of Thomas,* a collection of lost sayings of Jesus recently found in Egypt. In this Gospel James, brother of Jesus, the leader of the first Christian community in Jerusalem, is described by Jesus as the one 'for whose sake heaven and earth were created'.

With his census David did injury to the image of God. Human beings are not numbers, and can never 'add up' to a number; in this respect even the term 'manpower' is a perversion. God is mirrored in every human being — physically most clearly in the face. Hence the first in the second series of God's sayings concerning man appears where the Lord turns to an enraged Cain and says, 'Why are you angry and why has your countenance fallen?' (Gen.4:6).

To the first saying spoken by God concerning the human being we would add the words that immediately follow: divine thought created man 'male and female'

(Gen.1:27). The expression 'male and female' is an adverb, as though God had created man divided or 'two-sided'. The physical separation of woman from man occurred only later in paradise (Gen.2:22). In the world of the future this difference will no longer exist. In the Gospel of Matthew Jesus says, 'For in the resurrection they neither marry . . . but are like angels in heaven' (22:30). However, mankind, as it presently exists on the earth, needs this polarity. The reason for this will become clear when we come to the fifth saying.

2. The second saying concerning man is characterized as a blessing. God spoke: 'Be fruitful and multiply' (Gen.1:28). From the beginning, then, it was intended that mankind should be many. As will be found at the end of the three series this blessing is strengthened in the covenant with Abraham: 'I will multiply your descendants as the stars of heaven and as the sand which is on the seashore' (Gen.22:17).

In the Bible the stars were not thought of as randomly scattered through the night sky but as ordered, specifically in the twelve constellations or signs of the zodiac. Hence, Abraham's descendants were ordered 'as the stars of heaven' into the twelve tribes of Israel. The parallel branch of the family, the descendants of Ishmael, also reflected this order in the twelve bedouin princes (Gen.25:12–16).

In the time of the kings after David some of the individual tribes had already disappeared; in the Temple, however, the principle of the 'heavenly twelve' still ruled. When the turn came for priests from one of the lost tribes to serve in the Temple, descendants from these 'lost tribes' were simply called upon. Neither the size of any remaining remnant of the tribes nor the

weight of their political influence was of any consequence for the purposes of the Temple; heaven worked
through the twelve into the nation (Exod.24:4;
Num.13:2; Ezek.47:13ff; Zech.9:1).

Yet when the words of blessing over Abraham's descendants speak of 'the sand which is on the seashore'
just the opposite is the case. Here we *are* dealing with
the multitude, and it would be appropriate to ask how
many soldiers king David had at his disposal
(2Sam.24:2). But such an earthly census was only per-
missible if Israel's 'heavenly order' in the Temple had
already been assured. At the time of David's census,
that had not yet happened. Only afterwards did he
purchase land for the Temple.

For earthly purposes it is very necessary, though of
course of secondary importance, to know the exact
number of the multitude. Earthly power is founded
upon number. Oddly enough, it also affords social freedom to the individual. Only in the indefinite multitude
does an individual have the possibility to move about
freely. Such a field of freedom enables a person to decide
for *himself* where he wants to be without simultaneously injuring the heavenly order reflected in the
cultus, nation and mankind. The poet Stefan George
felt the indignity of this alienation from heaven when
he contemptuously said of a multitude of people,
'Already their number is a sin'. His comment applies to
those wanting to live only on the lower, earthly level of
human existence. Human beings in this category are in
constant danger of sinking down to an even lower level
of existence: the level of dust. The word 'dust' used in
the Bible as a picture for human beings signifies a stage
even lower than sand; for sand, which exists as discrete,
crystal grains, can at least be counted.

The divine command 'multiply, and fill the earth' justifies the multitude as a necessary, if lower, level of human existence. It enables the individual to be himself, wherever and however he wants, at least for a time, before he then settles down into a more enduring position in society, that is, before he finds a niche in life where only an indefinite investment of himself would have any meaning. In the long run everything depends on his finding such a life situation; for without the 'order of heaven' there is, for man, no lasting good, no eternal salvation.

3. The third saying tells man that the plants are to be his nourishment (Gen.1:29). Animal flesh is, for the life of the spirit, a problematic food. This is also true of wine or alcohol. According to the Bible, only since Noah (Gen.9:3f and 20f) has man been permitted to eat these substances. The misuse of human flesh for food would, in any case, mean certain spiritual ruin. Anyone desiring to raise himself to the level on which the first creation occurs, as described in the first chapter of Genesis, would do well to adopt the first advice given in the Bible concerning food and drink and not the advice later given to Noah.

4. The fourth saying concerning man (Gen.2:16–17) leads all the way down to the earth. The Lord signifies the trees in paradise as the appropriate source of nourishment and adds the limitation: 'but of the tree of the knowledge of good and evil you shall not eat, for on the day that you eat of it you shall die'.

For the first time evil and death are mentioned; this, even though the Fall had not yet occurred. However, as conceivable thoughts they were brought close to man.

Therefore it must not have been part of God's intention for mankind never to be touched in any way by these powers: rather only that evil should not enter the sphere of man's will. Death and evil should have remained standing, as it were, at the horizon of human consciousness, on the periphery of the theoretically possible, and from there exerted their influence. The Fall into sin occurring later allowed evil to slip into man, penetrating even into his will.

The danger is mentioned again in the second series of sayings where God warns Cain: 'And if you do not do well, sin is couching at the door; its desire is for you, but you must master it' (Gen.4:7).

For modern man the proper response for anyone feeling the forces of evil within himself is to contain them within himself without allowing them into the inmost region of his humanity, the region of the will. For if they are translated into actions that flow out into the world, then they have already entered this realm where the pure self lives. We are to guard and control our evil impulses, keeping them outside the door of our inner holy of holies. Then, encircled and contained by consciousness and wisdom, they can even be transformed into a powerful driving force for a life filled with strength, goodness and accomplishment.

Saul of Tarsus provides such an example. His initial rage to persecute the heretical Christian sects became, according to his constantly repeated witness, a driving force for his ministry through half the world as an apostle of Christ (1Cor.15:9f; Gal.1:13f; Eph.3:8; Phil.3:6–12). This is, however, only possible when Christ himself had become the center of the eternal human being, which lives deep in every personality (Rom.8:10). And this, then, is precisely what Augustine meant with his idea of a predestination that can reshape an entire life giving it new meaning.

5. In the fifth saying God says something rather strange about his own, as yet incomplete, work: 'It is not good . . .'! Up to now after every step of creation it had been stressed: 'And God saw that it was good'; now, however, the Lord says: 'It is not good that the man should be alone' (Gen.2:18). Immediately thereafter the snake approached the human being through woman. The separation of the human being into two sexes was the door through which the snake entered. Obviously the division was problematic and not without its dangers. And yet, as the fifth saying indicates, no separation at all would have been even worse. Individual man can easily become hardened in himself and turn into a 'windowless monad' as Leibniz expressed it. In speaking to Abraham God compares individual human beings with 'the sand which is on the seashore' (Gen.22:17). Human beings, however, sink even lower; the Bible then speaks of them as dust. That marks the loss not only of heavenly order but also of the clear, crystal hardness of grains of sand; mass-man has arrived.

God condemns the serpent to eat dust (Gen.3:14). Even man's physical body must sink into dust at death (Gen.3:19). The soul, on the other hand, should not follow this path. This is the path Mephistopheles planned for Faust: 'He shall eat dust and with enjoyment like my aunt the famous snake.' For mankind to sink to this level would mean the loss of eternity in the kingdom of God.

The very duality of the sexes saves many souls at an early stage from this form of destruction. The polarity of gender creates a gentle coercion, leading almost everyone to find his special 'thou'. If some people seek in the encounter not the 'thou' but the power of compulsion itself, then they are seeking disaster. They are then in danger of crossing the threshold from grain of sand to dust, which would signify their demise as a discrete spiritual entity, a human being. 'I and thou' form the first step of the ladder to heaven. Martin Buber was aware of this and never tired of praising the word 'thou' as the archetypal word of the Bible. 'Thou', when properly used in everyday life, can bring salvation to the person speaking it.

6. When God spoke concerning man for the sixth time, the Fall into sin had already occurred. Unfortunately, for reasons of space, we must forgo any discussion of this event itself. Our chosen line of development takes us next to the sixth saying: 'And they heard the sound of the LORD God walking in the garden in the cool of the day, and the man and his wife hid themselves from the presence of the LORD God among the trees of the garden' (Gen.3:8).

Today we hide ourselves in matter, just as Jesus said in the words of Hosea (10:8) concerning mankind at the end of the aeon. At that time humanity will once again experience the power of divine forces working directly into the realm of the earth. They will be terrified by these forces, to which they have long since grown unaccustomed, and 'then they will begin to say to the mountains, "fall on us"; and to the hills, "cover us" ' (Luke 23:30). The materialist's fear of the spirit of God began with Adam's hiding in the garden.

From his hiding place Adam at first heard only his name being called out by God. It was the first time he had heard it thus spoken (Gen.3:9). Because Adam's name came forth from the mouth of God in this way the spiritual existence of humanity was assured. Mankind would not be destroyed. An act of grace, this new mode of address blessed man despite the recent fall into sin. Even today this grace is still in effect. When God spoke the name 'Adam', it stood for *the human being,* for all human beings to follow. The universality of this name is found today in the word 'I', the name spoken by everyone for no-one but himself. Saying 'I' to oneself makes one a member of humanity, that is, one of Adam's descendants. Deep within the 'I' of every human being, God himself, the Creator, is still living. Because of this, modern man can find a sure path to God leading through the experience of the content of this name.

The word 'I' bears the free being of the self in the soul, the 'little spark of God' of which Meister Eckhart spoke. St Augustine and Johann Gottlieb Fichte, the little-known and much-underrated Idealist philosopher, also describe this path to God, the path of the responsible 'I'; it leads the inner self to open itself to the spirit above and then turn with devotion to the work of earth, the task of transforming this world we live in.

7. One question quickly follows another after Adam's name is called out: 'Where . . .? Who . . .? Have you . . .?' and in the seventh saying, spoken to Eve, finally also 'What is this that you have done?' (Gen. 3:13). Then God speaks to the serpent; he asks it no questions, but simply transfers it into another realm of existence. Through the different ways in which God deals with man and snake, we find another confirmation of the 'thou' in Adam.

8. The eighth and ninth sayings are curses from God; that is to say, faint-hearted people experience them as such. In reality they are, as all words from God, words of blessing. In this case, they indicate how man can master his destiny. To avoid any expression of bias in our terminology, we shall call them 'words of burden'. First God speaks to Eve: 'I will greatly multiply your pain in childbearing: in pain you shall bring forth children, yet your desire shall be for your husband, and he shall rule over you' (Gen.3:16).

9. The ninth saying is directed to the man *(adam)*: 'cursed is the ground [*adamah*] because of you; in toil you shall eat of it all the days of your life ... In the sweat of your face you shall eat bread till you return to the ground, for out of it you were taken; you are dust, and to dust you shall return' (Gen.3:17, 19).

The chief content of these sayings can be summarized in the words: pain and hard labor. Working at first with the effect of a curse upon mankind, these sayings remain a burden a long time; nevertheless, they can become the medicine of the soul, the cure for the fall from God which is called original sin.

10. The tenth saying summarizes the foregoing nine: 'Behold, the man has become as one of us ...' (Gen3:22).

The ten sayings follow the course of man's creation on earth. However, self-conscious human life, life of which we are personally aware, is found only at the last stage of creation. Therefore, it begins with the last of the ten sayings and works its way back through the earlier ones. Life, as we experience it, does not begin with the eternal decision of God, which preceded man's creation, but rather with the burden of work.

We have mastered life on the surface when we have at least found a good relationship to work. And the further we reach back through the divine sayings and make them our own, the deeper our soul life becomes. The human soul becomes mature to the extent that it actually accepts the suffering brought to it by life; it becomes deep as it wakens to the questions life presents to every human being and through them senses that God has a name for it, a name deriving from the realm of the eternal. The soul attains the full powers of earth when it has encountered evil and death without falling prey to them, and it will have the maturity for heaven when it has striven back to its source in God, from which all mankind springs.

1.8 Childhood and youth

I would like to discuss briefly how the elements of soul development mentioned relate to age in an individual's life. The creation of earthly mankind, as described in the Bible, covers childhood. Specifically, the creation of the body up to the point at which the Lord blew living breath into man (Gen.2:7) is parallel to the development in the embryo up to the first breath after birth. The book of Job (10:8–20) draws our attention to this fact. The expulsion from paradise, including the words of burden, is reflected in the threshold crossed around fourteen years of age. At this point, we must look in the other direction. To begin with, the young person must find his way to an independent relationship to work, to the enjoyment of work. Then he must master the remaining steps of divine sayings in reverse order until he hears his name spoken from God's own mouth; he will feel this and then 'know' the reason why he is on earth and what he should do. He will have spiritually come of age.

1.9 Work

'In the sweat of your face you shall eat bread' (Gen.3:19). Only when this, the ninth saying, is understood as a blessing and not as a curse can the life of a human being today develop in a healthy way. If it be assumed that one's 'personal life' begins tentatively with confirmation, as with David, then it becomes clear that everything depends on youth discovering the joy and satisfaction of work. Pre-Christian humanity was not yet aware of this. The psalmist sings, 'The years of our life are threescore and ten . . . yet their span is but toil and trouble' (Ps.90:10). Educated Greeks and Romans regarded handwork as beneath their dignity. Benedict of Nursia was the first to teach his Christian brothers: 'pray and work'. After him the same Psalm in Luther's translation sounded new and different: 'Our life lasts but seventy years, at the most eighty; and if it has been precious then it was toil and trouble'. Much more could be said concerning work, but space limits us to a brief discussion of a few further characteristics. The tilling of the soil by a man is the archetype of all work, but only the archetype. Of course it belongs, as does suffering, in equal measure to men and women. Work with the hands is the healthiest form of work for the soul. He neglects the training of his will who does not like to return to physical labor when forced by circumstances or when it is necessary to try out the best way of carrying out a task. On the other hand, he who does

35

physical work should not forget that properly done intellectual and spiritual work achieves much more for the world. The inventor of a much-needed device has already accomplished far more than a handworker, even though his contribution is also indispensable. Perhaps the proper science of man and his heavenly helpers accomplishes even more than any mere invention. In any case, work with the hands always exerts a healthy healing influence. Egypt, Greece and Rome used slave labor. The cities of the Christian Middle Ages made labor into a happy community activity. The Reformation and the Enlightenment — Kant too — considered work to be a personal duty or obligation to God and mankind. They regarded it as a rod needed by the soul for its salvation. Hard work, it was said, protects one from an 'impure life'.

In the nineteenth century, decisively in the second half, work came to be regarded more and more as a commodity, to be sold to the highest bidder. Today the 'labor market' is still with us. Yet there is little help for man in this view of work. Work will once again regain its full inner worth when it is motivated not by pay but flows from the joy of working and creating and from devotion to a larger whole. In this form, work will remain a characteristic of mankind for all times to come. Through Christ, the powers of blessing inherent in work can, with time, further unfold into a blossom of unexpected beauty. Yet, to begin with, only those souls who are prepared to carry God's words of burden can unite with Christ. Christ does not free us from suffering as Buddha attempted with his spiritual path, but he makes 'toil and trouble' fruitful for man so that he benefits from and is advanced by them in a way that is encouraging to behold.

1.10 Pain and suffering

A mother's pain during the birth of a child, during 'labor', is archetypal. For this reason, it elevates the woman above her personal and individual existence because it opens the way for another human being into life. Like labor pains, every pain and every consciously borne suffering can carry us beyond the limits of our natural selves. In the words of Meister Eckhart: 'There is no faster horse to carry one to the goal of perfection than suffering.' Only pain that has not been overcome or has been falsely interpreted leads to bitterness.

King David comes closest to the life of Christ in his suffering on the evening when he ran barefoot and crying through the garden (later to be known as Gethsemane) and up the Mount of Olives fleeing from his son Absalom and his treacherous adviser Ahithophel (2Sam.15:30). The same holds true for Paul in his trial before the Roman procurator in Jerusalem and Caesarea (Acts 21–27) and so also for many martyrs.

Pain and suffering lead us beyond the borders of the soul. For this reason alone, however, we are not allowed under any circumstances arbitrarily to set out to seek them. They can only be accepted. Of course, we sometimes must voluntarily undertake tasks which are dangerous or may be accompanied by pain. But only a consciousness above the human level can impart pain without becoming evil. And just as any earthly, arbitrary, avoidable application of pain is evil and always creates more evil up to the most horrible perversions of black magic, so, too, is any voluntarily self-inflicted injury also pathological. Because pain as such escapes earthly understanding, it can only be fruitfully overcome by a religious consciousness. Should suffering as a tester and guiding escort in the development of the human being become necessary, then it should only follow his having learned the joy of work and not be inflicted on him to any great degree beforehand. Destiny can do anything without injuring; for our benefit providence is allowed to break all the rules. However, as a rule, children and adolescents first need to find joy in a natural and harmoniously contoured existence; they need to find joy in their attempts at work and only later should they have to learn how to master serious suffering. As educators, we must strive to help them to find this joy in work and teach this first to the adolescents, otherwise the strength they need for life cannot take shape and grow in them.

The peoples of the East and the West have very different attitudes to work, to pain and suffering. In North America, nearly everyone enquires about the other person's work at every meeting; he asks what the other person is working on at the moment and often how much money is thereby earned. For the lazy or incompetent, this form of social intercourse can, psychologically speaking, take his breath away. In that land everyone wants to work. On the other hand, pain, suffering and death are strictly avoided in all casual conversation; they are hidden, suppressed and denied. One can make no sense of them.

In Eastern Europe work, the hard work which is, of course, also accomplished there, is experienced as compulsion, done seldom from one's own initiative. One complains that it is a form of suffering. However, almost everyone there is prepared to suffer and is also capable of suffering. Experiencing suffering, discussing it and holding up under it for long periods of time — in the East these all count as pre-eminently human.

In the European middle, between the West and the East, we have a unique opportunity to achieve a balanced relationship to both 'words of burden'. Mastering them creates forces in the soul which, when united, result in love in its most objective form. Everyone can test this for himself like an invisible chemical experiment carried out in the realm of the soul. Neither of the two forces is capable of doing it alone. Work alone can easily harden the human soul in egotism and a materialistic life; suffering by itself leads away from life or embitters one. Should these, or an even richer fusion (richer through the involvement of the other sayings of God which preceded these two), form the source of an active and at the same time enduring human love, then the spirit of Christ, by means of the same forces, can enter the soul, a soul which has awakened over long periods of history through the words of burden, the 'curse words', of God. The wisdom of the paradise myth can hardly be overestimated.

It is also food for thought that, compared with all the great, historically known founders of religions such as Moses, Zarathustra, Lao-tzu, Confucius, Buddha, Mani and Muhammad, only Jesus spent almost his entire life as a workingman. Furthermore, in his lifework alone suffering played an essential role which is not to be ignored.

We succeed on our path through life to the degree that these two words of burden (the will to work and the acceptance of suffering) become a second, higher nature within us. Nevertheless, we derive the fullest spiritual benefit from life when we take upon ourselves all ten of God's first sayings concerning man.

2 The Path through Life

2.1 The Creator of nature and the awakener of the self

Before beginning a discussion of biography as it presents itself to us in the guise of day-to-day living, I would like to comment on some other passages from Genesis which will give us further concepts for understanding it.

In Genesis, the names for God alternate. The science of Old Testament theology has based a theory on this alternation; it maintains that the text has been patched together from a number of more primary sources whose authors used different names for God. There is, as far as I can tell, no need for such a theory; the alternation makes sense and the sense in it is fruitful for an understanding of the laws that govern human life. The Hebrew story of creation in seven world days names the Godhead 'Elohim'. Although the word is in the plural, it governs a verb in the singular, with only the three exceptions already mentioned. And so we read 'In the beginning *God* created . . .' The description of paradise (Genesis 2–3) names God 'Yahweh-Elohim', which is translated with the 'LORD God' in the Revised Standard Version. Then, with the exception of a few parts of the expanded report of the Flood, God is afterwards called only 'Yahweh', the 'LORD' in the stories from Cain to Abraham. We shall leave out of our considerations the third name for God, 'El' with its various suffixes, which is used with Abraham in the Holy Land.

The change of the names follows a simple pattern: when the world and man are created, the text says

'Elohim', which we translate with 'God'; when the body of man as well as his consciousness is being formed, as in paradise, it says the 'LORD God'; and when the concern is only with human consciousness, as with Cain, we read only the 'LORD'. History and conscious biography are involved with the 'LORD'. Guilt and atonement, sin and forgiveness, the irregular elements in human biography, also belong with the 'LORD'. Although we are directing our attention to the regular phenomena that form the groundwork for and carry the irregular events in life, it is not primarily the 'creaturely' aspects of man that interest us. They would involve us with the name 'God'. We remain, then, with the 'LORD'.

Only in parts of the report of the Flood is the name 'Elohim' used again. That is understandable, for at that time God altered the physical earth; human consciousness was not involved. This intervention by a Creator became necessary because the paths of mankind were leading to a dangerous growth of bodily forces which were probably the result of occult eugenic machinations influencing man's genetic evolution. To this the Bible takes position with the following words: '. . . when the sons of God came in to the daughters of men, and they bore children to them. These were the mighty men that were of old, the men of renown . . . And the LORD was sorry that he had made man on the earth' (Gen.6:4, 6). When the work of the 'LORD', the awakener of human consciousness, was interfered with, the Godhead had to act once again as 'Elohim', that is, as nature Creator. Only in this way could the awakener of that consciousness which is specifically human maintain the upper hand. That was the spiritual cause of the Flood. The 'LORD' also shortened man's life span (Gen.6:3) thereby moving death into man's consciousness and creating the order of the changing seasons (Gen.9). After the Flood it was once again the 'LORD' alone who accepted Noah's offering (Gen.8:20ff).

In the stories of the patriarchs, it is the Creator-name, 'Elohim', that always appears when the text is concerned with the generations. It also appears, for the first time in its complete form, when Moses heard the words 'the God of Abraham, the God of Isaac, and the God of Jacob'. Here God is called 'Elohim', even though only 'the LORD' is used in the rest of this section dealing with the burning bush on Mount Sinai (Exod.3). Genesis and Exodus both employ the various names for the Godhead strictly following the distinction described above. From the burning bush, however, Moses hears a new self-characterization of God. This name leads in a direction which by now has become clear. From the fire he hears 'I AM WHO I AM' or 'I WILL BE WHAT I WILL BE', which could also be translated in accordance with its meaning: 'I am at the disposal of no-one and there is no way I can be commanded; however, I approach you human beings again and again, always revealing and acting in a new and different way.'

In Jerusalem the name 'Yahweh' was forbidden except in its role in the Temple ritual which would otherwise have been occupied by a cultic image or picture. The priest spoke the holy name only there, and only at special times during the offering service in order to invoke the presence of God. In the less important ceremonies held in the Temple, the priest probably called out or sang, instead of the holy name 'Yahweh', the word *ani-hu,* which we translate as 'I am'. This is the great 'I am' spoken only by the Godhead.

In John's Gospel Christ often relates this self-designation of God to himself; and the text of

Matthew's Gospel also makes it probable that Jesus answered with the cultic *ani-hu* when in court where the high priests asked him to swear by the living God, 'tell us if you are the Christ, the Son of God'. The court understood this as blasphemy (Matt.26:63f).

Even the name 'Yahweh', the 'LORD', the linguistic significance of which is uncertain, is often used in the Old Testament to signify God as 'I'. In accordance with this, the Ten Commandments begin, not with the usual *ani* but with the emphatic form of the first person pronoun: *anokhi Yahweh eloheykha,* literally, 'I, I am the Lord, your God'. Under the light of this revelation, as under a heavenly umbrella, the 'I' of mankind was slowly developed.

The short forms of the unutterable name are *Yah* and *Yo. Yo* stands at the beginning of personal names and *Yah* at their end, as in *Johanan* and *Elijah*. It is interesting to note that both of these forms only came to mean 'I' in European languages in Christian times: in Italian and in modern Greek as *io,* and in Slavic as *ja.* The German word for 'I', *ich,* is derived from the Old German word *ek,* and took the form of the initials 'Jesu Christi'. (*I, J* and *Y* are interchangeable, as they each come from the Hebrew *yod* and Greek *iota.*)

The 'I' of God forms the main theme of the Bible up to the appearance of Jesus. This 'I' was the 'portion of Jacob' (Jer.10:16). In its glow, consciousness was ripened to awareness of a history in Israel which takes on shape like an organic whole in which nothing reappears exactly the way it was. In the light of this 'portion', a word which could also be translated as 'treasure', the biographical consciousness of individual human beings could also ripen. Hidden under this new awareness of history and of individual biography, the human 'I' itself, which makes up the core of every biography, grew and matured. Augustine, who discovered the essence of biography, was also the first to coin the philosophical expression for this spiritual center of the human being: 'the I', *'ego, ego animus'* (*Confessions*, X 6.9).

Of course, the word 'I' or 'ego' can be used thoughtlessly in psychology and even more so in everyday life. This must be borne in mind. In everyday life, however, there is a good remedy against the false use of the word: working in the service of others. The great *ani-hu* spoken by Christ can be clearly heard speaking through the small 'I' of the human being to the extent that calling, duty and service are hidden in our concept of 'I'. In the end, it is only through Christ's 'I am' that our lives attain spiritual weight and can grow into eternity. John never ceases saying the same thing again and again in the Gospel; Paul, too, in his letter to the Romans (8:9–11). Such secrets lie hidden in the 'portion of Jacob'.

2.2 *The power of death to shape*

When Jesus spoke the divine *ani-hu* as a man, he brought death upon himself. He did not attract it as a fate external to himself, rather he did something much more: he took it into his very being. In a far more limited way this secret is woven into every human biography.

Seen from the point of view of the Bible, death appears as the consequence of sin (Gen.2:17); and as Paul says, 'the wages of sin is death' (Rom.6:23). However, just as the words of burden concerning work and suffering can become words of blessing, so too can death have a blessing effect. For it is only death and our awareness of death that give us a gauge to judge where we stand in life. The awareness of death lends significance to every moment we live; it compresses our life content. Death gives life contours, it creates man's *Zeitgestalt*.

According to the Bible, the patriarchs lived many centuries, a claim we will not evaluate at this point. Methuselah, with 969 years, lived longest. Only Enoch found a balanced measure for his years: from the sun he took the number 365. He and Elijah are the only figures to whom the Old Testament attributes an ascension into heaven (Gen.5:24, 2Kings 2:11). In the old Jewish legends, Moses appears as a third figure with these two.

Before the Flood, the Lord at first wanted to heal mankind from its sins by shortening its lifespan; he curtailed man's overgrown physical form by severely compressing the time dimension of his life. The text says, 'My spirit [breath, or fire] shall not abide in man for ever, for he is flesh, but his days shall be a hundred and twenty years' (Gen.6:3). Before this event, man's life-expectancy had exceeded human consciousness, just as it does today, in a healthy way, in children. For a child, a single year, not to mention a lifetime, is so endlessly long that it is unsurveyable. Death does not yet give a child any stimulus for life, and once it was the same for all mankind. According to the Bible, this was different after Noah. Expressed in terms of modern natural science, this change occurred immediately after the last Ice Age, between 10 000 and 8 000 BC. Only Moses lived exactly seventy years according to the Bible. The present-day standard of seventy years is mentioned only once in the entire Old Testament, in the Ninetieth

Psalm, and refers specifically to David the King. It is not a coincidence that David also provides us with the first life history which can be considered, without qualification, to be a biography in the present-day sense of the term.

2.3 Elijah and Jezebel

The sinful impulse, which caused the life forces to proliferate during Noah's time, continued working long after. During the time of the kings in Israel, the people gathered around the fertility god Baal. This stream of worship reached a peak of self-awareness under Queen Jezebel of Samaria. Under the name of Baal, the patron god of her homeland, this princess from Sidon gathered together all those who believed in blood and soil. Her opponent in the service of the Lord was Elijah the prophet. In 1Kings 18:38 we find a description of their encounter. Calling down the lightning of the 'LORD' upon his offering in a contest with the rain-making priests of Baal, Elijah emerged the victor. Elijah saw human souls as created by spirit and coming from above; Jezebel saw them as only natural and as produced from below. She wanted to cultivate the human race through inheritance; he wanted a strengthening and awakening of consciousness. She was concerned only with powers deriving from birth and these only in the coarsest sense without the spiritual perspectives concerning birth and childhood provided by the story of creation, the Book of Job, and so on. In the first chapter we discussed the birth–death polarity of human life and the forces that emanate from it. Elijah was concerned with the forces radiating from the death pole of life; with divine powers that could awaken human beings to the fact of their sin, to the life of the spirit and ultimately to themselves.

At this time Jehoshaphat was sitting on the throne of David in Jerusalem. Before he became king in 874 BC, Judah and Israel, the two states created when David's kingdom was divided after Solomon's death in 932 BC, had been at war for sixty years. Jehoshaphat made peace with Samaria by taking Jezebel's daughter, Athaliah, back to Jerusalem as crown-princess for his eldest son. Jehoshaphat either did not know about Elijah and his work or he simply paid no attention to him. The new daughter-in-law, however, seemed to know well enough what was at stake. Furthermore, she had her own intentions for the future spiritual life in Judah. She sought to implement her plans by introducing the worship of Baal into the southern kingdom and attempting to purge the messianic line from the throne in Jerusalem.

Jehoshaphat's fatal naivety with respect to Jezebel and Athaliah was inevitable because he lacked any sense for the power of death to shape and form personality. His betrayal of Elijah, which was probably the result of unconscious stupidity, was also caused by this lack. At this time, Elijah was to be found on Mount Sinai in the same caves in which Moses had seen God. There he received the mission of his life, a threefold command of death and ruin: '. . . you shall anoint Hazael to be king over Syria; and Jehu . . . to be king over Israel; and Elisha . . . to be prophet in your place' (1Kings 19:15). These commandments led Syria to war with Israel; they threw Israel into internal confusion and turmoil which introduced her collapse, and they cast their courageous recipient, Elijah, under the shadow of death. Elijah was the first in Israel to bear his death — in this case a very early one — in full consciousness, with courage born of religious strength. In doing so, he reached a step on the ladder of ascent where God's 'threat of death' heard in paradise is transformed into a blessing. The complete and final transformation of death later became a possibility for every human being as a result of the death and resurrection of Jesus.

Birth and death, the polar forces of our lives which work in a regular fashion, have now been sufficiently described for our present purposes. We turn, then, to the various stages of life.

2.4 Rhythms

The most regular phenomena of our lives lie in the short rhythms of the body: heartbeat and breath. Longer rhythms of life are created by the earth and the sun as day and night. Man answers day and night with waking and sleeping. The round-dance of the seasons forms the next stage. Our body's need for this rhythm is not always as clear as the need for it in the plant world; but even in man, disturbances caused by illness point to this dependence. In the religious life, the rhythm of the sun is consciously strengthened by means of the great festivals.

Breath, day and year are closely related, for together they determine, oddly enough, the possible length of our lives. As many breaths as we take in one day is approximately the number of days in our life, that is, as many years as the Ninetieth Psalm grants us, seventy to eighty or a little more. And the number of days found in seventy-two years is the number of years required for the sun's vernal equinox to move through all the signs of the zodiac. This length of time is called a Platonic Year. It is explained astronomically as a slow precession of the earth's axis which, when observed only through the course of a single year, appears to be standing still. The number common in all these correspondences is 26 000, approximately. According to the teaching of Rudolf Steiner, a human being also reincarnates in accordance with this Platonic Year. In every world month, the human being incarnates once as a man and once as a woman. Incarnations would accordingly occur about a thousand years apart; today often more frequently. That is also the same span spoken of in the Ninetieth Psalm: 'For a thousand years in thy sight are but as yesterday when it is past, or as a watch in the night.' Man usually rushes a little ahead of the earth and its rhythms; he is in a hurry. Nevertheless, man and earth in all their recurring phenomena form an elastic, pendulating unity, a single being vibrating with life.

Year, day, and Platonic Year we leave aside now and turn to our chief concern: the chronological structure of life, man's *Zeitgestalt*. Here a seven-year rhythm prevails. The greatest doctor of Greek times, Hippocrates of Cos, pointed to this fact as early as 460 BC.

The child's body undergoes a radical change of form in the seventh and in the fourteenth years. The transformation in the soul life of the child at these times is equally great. While the physical changes in form pretty much disappear in the following multiples of seven (21, 28, 35 and so on), further steps in the development of the soul life clearly continue. The human soul with its many distinguishable though inseparable aspects continues to unfold throughout life. The first seven years of life contain more secrets than all the remaining years together. Jean Paul, the poet, remarked that this is true for the first three years alone. These seven years belong more to the development of the body, the basis for the person's future soul life, than to the conscious unfolding of the individual personality. They constitute a world for themselves, existing in the realm of unconscious creation, the world of the Godhead working as 'Elohim' rather than as the 'LORD'.

2.5 The second seven years

Almost the same holds for the second period of childhood between the seventh and the fourteenth years. The child no longer teaches himself exclusively through the senses; he now employs more than imitation to rise into his humanity. Using words he is able now to hear about and learn things which by himself he would never have been able to experience; for example, the history of ages past. At this stage, however, judgments and evaluations requiring independent thought are left to his parents and teachers.

The child is brought up and taught in groups; a situation he finds most comfortable. He wants to be like, speak like, be dressed like and be handled like all the other children he knows. He experiences himself primarily as a member of his age group, not yet really as an individual. In the strict sense of the word he does not yet have a biography. The portrayal of this stage of life we leave, therefore, to those trained in pedagogy. Bearing in mind that the paradise story, with its stages of human development, reflects the first fourteen years of life and that the independent human being must go through these steps in reverse order, we turn now to the age at which individuals take their first major steps towards independence.

2.6 Youth

The age at which an individual can begin to take his own life in hand and consciously guide it is fourteen years. This step can be supported with the Sacrament of Confirmation.

Whenever possible adolescents join together to form small 'packs' with their own unique customs. Teenagers, whose souls have received too little nourishment, tend to form very loose groups which quickly come together and quickly separate again. Such volatility is not ideal; for actually these groups of from five to twenty individuals provide the first experience of a higher social entity outside the family. This phenomenon belongs exclusively to the teenage years; human beings usually arrive in the world, if you will forgive the expression, 'in batches' and depart again the same way. The saying of God, 'It is not good that man should be alone' (Gen. 2:18) is reflected in this phenomenon as well as in the institution of marriage.

There comes a time when every adolescent wants to separate himself, at least partially, from his parents and previous teachers and seek a new authority. During this transition he often becomes very isolated and lonely. He is not able to be alone by himself for any length of time and is by no means strong enough yet to live solely from his own soul forces. At this stage he only possesses the freedom of choice; not yet real freedom, which can be described as the freedom to create out of oneself — the freedom of invention.

Any newfound leader is idolized, that is, hopelessly overestimated, as long as the youth reveres him. Yet for his further development he absolutely needs older people whom he can revere. Of course, as soon as an adolescent begins to criticize he immediately grossly underestimates. In younger children he usually sees only inability, in those older than himself either angels and heroes or devils and weaklings; not really any human beings yet. He is not yet able to accept people the way they are. On the other hand it is now (particularly in the fourth year of this seven year period) possible for him to feel and experience more from the sphere of the angels than will probably ever again be possible.

An oft appearing tragedy that belongs to the realm of forces working irregularly into life often begins in these years. Through immature attitudes and uncontrolled emotional reactions the life situation of later years is unfavorably predisposed. This can happen, for example, through poor school attendance, senseless spite or premature departure from home. Here regularity is found only in the fact that such regrettable occurrences appear in the third seven year period. It appears we are fated to forge the greatest part of our destiny at a time when we are least capable of knowing what we are doing. Behind this riddle lies real artistic technique in the creation of biography; as Hegel would say, a trick of heavenly reason.

In early adolescence everything depends on the young man or woman finding personal initiative to work. We have already spoken of the benefits of physical work for the health of the soul — tilling the soil is the archetype of all physical labor. Next must come an even more important labor: work on the invisible field which we call the soul. Much must be sown in this field, that is, learned, although one knows that the decisive sowing and harvesting will only take place much later. The soil is now tilled, lupin and other good herbs are sown and then ploughed under again. A fertile 'top soil' must be built up for the really important crops of the future. What they will be, no one knows. Therefore, an unnecessarily early or even final specialization in the course of study should be avoided.

2.7 Work

The danger is very great today that many young people will not find a taste for hard work; neither for physical work nor for the work of the mind known as learning; to say nothing of the higher form of work accomplished when the mind is engaged in the activity known as research. What Johnny doesn't learn now, that is, how to learn, he will, as the saying goes, never learn. Here the danger is very great; the meaning of life is in jeopardy. If a young man or woman has not learned to work by age eighteen then immediate and effective help from others is in order.

In my experience an effective remedy in such cases is a year-long stay in North America. Not, of course, as a visit for sightseeing but in order to work and earn money. If the duration is limited to one year then the young person has a chance to be fully penetrated by the good work-climate present there, but the weakness of this culture, its fear of suffering for example, will not have time to work too deeply into the soul.

There are, of course, many ways to train the will and learn to work. Today, however, the observation is unpopular that service as a soldier a hundred years ago did, indeed, help many young men whose weak wills needed strengthening. But only a few were able to transform the military training of the will into something personal, which then became an integral part of their own personality. This training remained, from the point of view of the individual, problematical. But it helped, at least, to fill a void that should not be allowed to exist. A stay in America can serve to strengthen young people in a similar way but, all things considered, does more. More is experienced and, in any case, by then it is time to leave the parents' home.

We have already discussed the history of work in our culture. Western man is now at a stage where the earlier incentives, survival of the fittest, hunger and materialistic egotism, often no longer provide sufficient grounds for initiative. Even ambition and social ascent are losing their force. People usually allow themselves to be unconsciously carried along by the old incentives preserved by force of habit. In austerely run states, be they fascistic or communistic, fear of punishment still plays a big role as inducement to work. In America it is fear of want and loss of social stature. But all these incentives from the past are losing their power. For the future a rich field of possible motivation is found in the knowledge of the potential development of the individual in the course of life, the knowledge of attainable goals with their appropriate stages and possible omissions. Just as important will be the knowledge of those psychic abilities that are more and more becoming attainable for all mankind; new qualities of soul which, until now, were incapable of being developed, are now becoming necessary for humanity.

The study of biography provides us with a first step in finding motivation for life. This study can help the individual find rewarding goals both for his life and for the culture of the present. The joy to be found in work, whether it be work of the past or any modern form thereof, will remain the foundation upon which the human soul keeps itself lively and adaptable. Without this flexibility there can be no inner development. Goethe hinted at this foundation stone when he said: 'The first thing we ask a man is: "What do you do?" the second: "With whom do you associate?" '

2.8 *Pain and suffering*

The first ten sayings of God concerning man will now serve us as a guide along the path which a soul travels through life. In Genesis they occur in the sequence:
1. The image of God
2. The great number
3. Nourishment
4. Death and evil
5. Name
6. Questions
7. Questions
8. Suffering
9. Work
10. Summation of the foregoing nine: 'Behold, the man has become like one of us, knowing good and evil' (Gen.3:22).

We are discussing the sequence in reverse order and have already dealt with work and suffering. We now continue with the problem of pain and suffering. In earlier ages tribes inflicted great pain on boys during their youth initiations; among the Greeks this practice survived with the Spartans. Although this is no longer appropriate, adolescents in this age group today still treasure opportunities for a very simple, even rough existence. Although we should make it possible for them to find such opportunities, it is equally important for us to exercise caution so that no serious illness or injury results from youth's natural lack of a sense for limits.

Camps in the wilderness are maintained in America in recognition of this need.

In earlier times the artistic imagination of girls received a training at this age. The power of artistic fantasy to form and shape, possessed by all young children, usually collapses at puberty. This is a widely known fact. Their music and painting make this obvious to the ear and eye. Artistic ability must be developed anew. Fortunately, this can be relatively easily achieved through theater and acting experiences; indeed, the value of acting experience for the development of the soul in this age group cannot be overestimated. Of course, the other fine arts should also eventually return, both in boys and girls. In ages past girls learned to spin, weave and sew; in the last century they at least still learned to sew well. Perhaps today they should be allowed to design and tailor their own clothes more often. In this way they would each have the opportunity to reveal their soul just as they choose, through the conscious choices and the workmanship of self-made clothing. Such an activity works in a powerful way shaping and creating the personality, the very soul itself.

As nature would have it, more pain is waiting in life for girls than for boys. On this point we can rely on nature and destiny to have their say. But the strength necessary to accept and bear up under suffering can be acquired, at least a beginning can be made, through a religious education. The Jewish and Christian religions have devoted a great deal of attention to this side of life. But it is important in our day to follow the proper sequence of steps; the will to work must not be jumped over and hence be left undeveloped. Such an omission could result from a one-sided religious education. The proper rule is: we want to work, and we bear pain and suffering which come to us though we do not want them.

2.9 The great questions

The questions raised in the two preceding sayings, why, who, how, and where, arise by themselves in adolescence. These questions need time to ripen. At first the answers seek only to be felt in and through artistic activity. This slow process of maturation makes it possible for them to appear later on all the more clearly in articulate words and confident actions.

In some cases it is helpful in searching for these answers to study carefully the beginnings of European philosophy. Perhaps at first only Greek mythology, then the sayings of Heraclitus and finally some Plato. The real desire for philosophical inquiry does not awaken until the nineteenth year. From then on there are no ideas fundamental to life or science that should remain closed to a young person — so far as his inclination and abilities reach. At this age the act of thinking can best be learned from Plato, a fact which does not exclude Fichte and other thinkers. In German-speaking countries Fichte's public speeches still possess an uncommon power to awaken.

Anthroposophy can only be beneficially taken up by young people who are ready and disposed to engage in philosophy; that is, beginning at nineteen years and under no circumstances before the eighteenth year. Otherwise Anthroposophy becomes just like other philosophical systems swallowed by sixteen- and seventeen-year-olds: dogmatism. However, every dogmatic philosophy paralyzes the life of thought, even though one who swallows a philosophic system without adequate chewing may well feel himself to be enriched thereby. Should the system be all-encompassing and embrace much of the world then the paralyzing effect is not noticed. The young person is sufficiently satisfied with setting prefabricated thoughts into motion. He is intoxicated by this newly discovered world of ideas and concepts which can be moved about and joined together in various combinations. On the other hand, a dogmatic world view with genuine spiritual origins may represent for many souls and throughout their lives, all that is possible and therefore proper. But then it should be cultivated within the framework of a religious life that expresses itself chiefly in the development of feeling and the ennobling of will impulses.

2.10 *The discovery of the self*

The chief question for the young person is, of course, the question of his own spiritual being. What is the name actually spoken by God? The question takes many forms: Who am I? What do I want? What should I do in the world? Around age seventeen or eighteen girls often answer this question all too easily by changing their names. This may, of course, be appropriate but caution is called for. Changing one's name works deeply into the soul. For young men an important aspect of the question is answered through their choice of profession.

2.11 *Face to face with death*

The question of name reaches into the realm of the 'I', the true ego, in the best spiritual sense. It can only be asked fruitfully when simultaneously the willingness awakens to include also the next saying of God, the words concerning death. This is especially true for the young man. To have looked death in the face gives self-confidence, creates big-hearted generosity and awakens the power of sacrifice. It readily awakens in young people an idealism and piety of an intensity that is seldom seen at any other stage of life and rarely displayed today. According to Plato (beginning of the *Republic* and elsewhere) devotion and reverence provide the foundation for all the other virtues which everything in life depends upon. This healthy piety gives the soul a felt worth and moral weight that allows it increasingly to overcome selfishness as the years pass.

Only an individual can look death in the eye. Devotion, on the other hand, is fostered best in a community of appropriate size. Especially conducive to this end are groups consisting of a hundred or more young people all of the same age. It is important for youth today that such occasions be created. Religious ritual also provides an especially pure means of meeting this need. Such a healthy and sober form of piety helps make possible a proper spiritual development in later life.

Through an encounter with death the young man is attempting to achieve something which the young woman usually experiences a little later in a different and more natural way either in her first enduring love or more often in the birth of her first child. The young man then finally finds the opportunity to catch up with the girls who had run away from him in the first years of teenage development.

That death and love belong together at the age of nineteen and are actually related to one another is witnessed too in many folk songs, and also in the ancient mysteries, particularly the Eleusinian. Both sexes experienced these mysteries for the first time at this age and decorated themselves, as if betrothed, with crowns of myrtle leaves. Crowns and garlands for the dead were also made from the branches of another species with somewhat larger leaves. Today this species is still called in German *Totenmyrtle,* which means 'death myrtle'. With respect to their form the mysteries were similar to a wedding. A voluntary death was to be inwardly experienced and overcome. Apuleius (AD 120) therefore named it 'the marriage of death'.

In coarser times than ours battles were still fought 'personally', for example during the Crusades. Those wars had only the name in common with the insane destructions we have witnessed in the twentieth century. In those days one could have said for a young man: every generation needs its war. If this sentence is understood only as describing a situation for a soul then it is possible to admit the truth in it. Today, as a substitute for this need, we have hang gliders, sailing on the open sea, mountain climbing, or, in Germany, expiation service in Israel with hard labor. Such service is good. All shirking on the other hand leads to ruin for the masculine soul.

The involvement of many young people in drugs in our time comes, as far as I can see, in no small measure from the fact that our civilization prevents them from engaging their strength in truly important struggles that are literally a matter of life and death. The well-known tendency toward suicide in this age-group (eighteen to twenty-one) also arises from the necessity of this encounter with death. When practised with true devotion the fine arts can reach so deeply into that part of the soul where the will forces reside that they blunt the dangerous spike of the dramatic crises so often unavoidable at this age. Everything is then shaped much more harmoniously.

This important step in development can also be described more inwardly and on a higher plane. Exactly at eighteen years, seven months and four days the first moon node is either fulfilled or resolved. On that day the moon node (the crossing of the moon's path with the ecliptic) returns to the same position relative to the earth and sun which it had when the human being was born. Anyone who has carefully observed the ebb and flow of the life forces in his own body knows that they resonate in many ways with the rhythms of the moon; at least, with a rhythm having the same length as the moon. Body and soul are bound together by moon forces. At the time when the moon nodes occur a part of the soul forces separates from the body and can then open itself to the objective spirit in the world and place itself at its disposal. In this or that person there occurs a kind of enlightenment during the night; a little naturally-occurring initiation. In early Christian times it was interpreted as a conversion. Indeed, this age of life has always been marked by numerous conversions.

2.12 The first moon node

We remain awhile with the saying of God concerning death: 'of the tree of the knowledge of good and evil you shall not eat, for in the day that you eat of it you shall die' (Gen.2:17). Despite this warning the fall into sin occurred soon afterwards. In the wake of the Fall the Lord first ordained a punishment for the snake with the words: 'upon your belly you shall go, and dust you shall eat all the days of your life. I will put enmity between you and the woman, and between your seed and her seed; he shall bruise your head, and you shall bruise his heel' (Gen.3:14–15).

The consequence is described at its fully developed stage in the main section of the Book of Revelation:

> And a great portent appeared in heaven, a woman clothed with the sun, with the moon under her feet, and on her head a crown of twelve stars; she was with child and she cried out in her pangs of birth, in anguish for delivery. And another portent appeared in heaven; behold, a great red dragon ... stood before the woman who was about to bear a child, that he might devour her child when she brought it forth; she brought forth a male child, one who is to rule all the nations with a rod of iron, but her child was caught up to God and to his throne, and the woman fled into the wilderness ... And ... the dragon ... pursued the woman who had borne the male child ... The serpent poured water like a river out of his mouth after the woman, to sweep her away with the flood. (Rev.12:1–6; 13–16).

These and certain other accompanying pictures can become the content of an enlightenment. They appear quickly and are full of movement, furthermore they need not always be seen in their completeness. They can also appear quite independently; the person experiencing these pictures need not have known them from the Bible.

The woman in this apocalyptic scene is known in theology as the apocalyptic Madonna. It is, at the same time, a picture of the soul on the higher level upon which it maintains itself for a few moments during the enlightenment. During these few moments the dragon is temporarily covered up or driven out. A pure stratum of the soul that otherwise lies hidden then appears. This is an undamaged substratum of the soul, the common possession of all mankind, friendly to the body without being bound to it and still able to reach up to heaven.

Afterwards the dragon attempts to drown the pure soul in a great stream of excess lower bodily forces. As a consolation the Apocalypse adds the picture of the earth itself coming to the aid of the pure soul and swallowing these bodily forces. The picture of the desert shows that this part of the soul is, for the time being, not available in everyday life. Until then the words spoken to Cain from the second series of ten sayings applies: 'sin is couching at the door; its desire is for you, but you must master it' (Gen.4:7).

The vision which was revealed to young people of this age in favorable instances in the ancient Eleusinian mysteries corresponded to the visions which are sometimes released today by the first moon node. At the high point of those sacred ceremonies, around midnight of the ninth day, the hierophant called out under the great fire: 'The virgin has borne a child, strength to the strong!' This goddess, Persephone, rode in a wagon pulled by a dragon.

2.13 Spiritual development

Following the first ten sayings of God, we now leave the paradise story and enter the preceding six days of creation. At the same time we leave the visible world and return to an older invisible stage of creation. If we wanted to follow this path even further back, it would become hidden or 'occult'. It includes a saying concerning spiritually appropriate nourishment, another concerning the secret of the great number and, tacitly, concerning number altogether, that is, the Many, the Four, the Three, and as the deepest secrets, the Two and the One. Finally there follows the saying which names man as the image of God.

Within the bounds of biography we cannot describe the occult path. The Book of Job compared with the first chapter of Genesis would help us sooner than anything else. Plato, the cabbala, and Fichte in his *The Way towards the Blessed Life (Anweisung zum seligen Leben)* of 1806 would further help us to unveil the secrets of number in the foundation of the world. A first door to the understanding of such secrets is presented by the vision possible at the time of the first moon node. For many young people the door to heaven is opened just a crack in the short span of time between the eighteenth and twenty-first years. Fortunately many decisions concerning future professions are made in these years before the individual has fully descended into his earthly self. At this point a decision illuminated by even one ray of heavenly light will likely hold for life. It is, however, still possible that life itself does not allow this decision to be carried out. If this happens, then a tragic mood enters one's life. Such a mood of sadness, however, works to keep the soul in touch with heaven. It remains religious and, from above, God sees its plight.

2.14 *The twenties*

There is a soft expression that can often be seen in the eyes until the age of twenty-one. It now disappears; the eyes become firm, as if they had crystallized just a little. Now it is high time to leave the parents' home. The natural powers of the intellect are at their height during the fourth seven-year period. The power of thinking is easiest to awaken at this time. This is also the best time for a young man or woman to learn about the world; the ideal time for seeing the world. The individual enriches his spirit as the mind and soul are filled with experience. It is time to conquer the universe of the intellect and the world of sense experience. Happy is he who can preserve his youthful devotion and reverence during this necessary exploration. As a pure, suprapersonal element this reverence can be woven into the very fabric of his soul life. In no way is this contradicted by Goethe when he says: 'Piety is not a goal but a means for achieving the highest culture through pure peace of soul.' When considering how a soul can develop most fruitfully, it makes no sense to speak of 'two paths', the one religious, the other a more intellectual path of individual spiritual striving. A mood of devotion regularly stimulated and nurtured by the purity of suprapersonal ritual can remain an effective means of spiritualization throughout life. On the other hand it must also be said that exacting mental and spiritual work is the highest that a human being can achieve by himself on this earth. Combining the efforts of both powers of the soul, the head and the heart, will always be fruitful, their separation always unfruitful.

Along with the two-path theory, young people often construct a second obstacle for themselves. They feel very strongly the tension between their education, or whatever their particular occupational training may be named, and spiritual concepts and exercises. At first they attempt to bridge this gulf by dedicating themselves to their training and saving their spiritual efforts for a later stage in life. But the human being travels each of these paths with his entire soul, and any path followed will affect the soul as a whole. The soul of a human being can be separated into several departments without suffering injury, even if the departments are separated only by time. What can be done with the span of a day, however, cannot be duplicated with the course of a lifetime. This general rule is not altered by the fact that any individual destiny can so dispose without causing injury. When one comes to know or even suspect the moral worth of a course of action, then he must immediately so direct his desires and efforts. Healing and salvation lie in living with both ways of learning, in feeling them to be, in fact, opposites and yet continuing to live with the constant struggle. The great effort called forth by this tension will always serve to strengthen the person.

It must never be forgotten during the lofty flights of the twenties that real experience with the forces of the earth and mankind are still not present. The faculties for understanding the world must first grow and become clarified; only later can action on a large scale based on one's own judgment follow. Again Goethe says quite accurately in *Sprüche in Prose:* 'On the average, knowledge determines the man ... his commissions and omissions; for this reason there is nothing more dreadful to see than ignorance in action.'

2.15 *Marriage*

At twenty-five the human being achieves a new stage of maturity, the first real maturity of adulthood. As a craftsman he can now become a master; correspondingly, he can now work independently in almost all occupations. A young man in such circumstances should also consider the possibility of marriage. In the old days that was prescribed for the young master within one year. According to old Christian customs a young man of this age could become a priest. Of course, this now also applies to women.

For a young woman the thought of marriage is now

entirely appropriate. She should not begin a marriage under any circumstances before the first completed moon node; if at all possible, not before the twenty-first year. When wives over forty come to psychiatrists with the idea that their husbands are becoming alienated, the first question they are usually asked, and with good reason, is: 'At what age did you marry?' All too often they did a great injustice to their lives twenty years before by marrying too young. They never had a chance to awaken fully to themselves as individuals. Only someone who is securely anchored in himself can trust others. The maturity of at least twenty-one years is necessary for this inner security.

2.16 *The will awakens*

At twenty-eight no one wants to study any more, at least not as a chief occupation. Most people would now like to have finally begun their life-work. It is important to know this when planning a course of training: study becomes more and more a torture after twenty-eight. In the Egyptian mythology reported to us by Plutarch the god Osiris was killed in his twenty-ninth year. After his death he ruled over the dead. The old Egyptian initiation represented the completion of the required course of study for the rising generation of rulers. The contents of this initiation accompanied the soul into the kingdom of the dead; in the sleep of the mysteries every adept followed his god of the same age into the lower worlds. Afterwards the graduates were sent out to serve the country.

It was also at this age that Gautama Buddha in India renounced the world in which he would otherwise have become king. After that he wandered through the world as an ascetic, educating himself under the direction of masters of inner contemplation. Then at thirty-five he found his own unique enlightenment. He discovered it, unlike other protected and carefully led adepts, entirely within himself and on a level so high as to have been previously unknown.

2.17 The thirties

The thirties bring the first real opportunity to compare one's own accomplishments with those of others. In the business world this usually occurs through a comparison of personal income. Only now is the question justified which the individual puts to the general public, 'What am I worth to you?' Now wages can increase from year to year and from position to position. The family is usually large enough now to use up father's well-earned money in a morally salutary fashion. A family house, particularly for the sake of the children, is much to be desired at this time.

Money, will, and 'results-oriented' activity are always closely related. Therefore, those still in their twenties are endangered when they are paid high salaries and wages; the will is called forth prematurely. In this way the proper education of the feelings and the development of the mind are hindered and these faculties can only be fully awakened in the twenties. All too often young people are crippled in their soul life through excessively high wages.

Astonishingly enough a similar injustice is sometimes committed by people otherwise alert to the principles of soul development. This error occurs when they send young people who are teachable and willing to learn into full occupational employment in their early twenties assuring them of opportunities to further their education at a later date. Life's stages are not interchangeable; they are firmly ordered. In the twenties we develop primarily feelings, thoughts and theoretical knowledge; in the thirties the will. In the thirties the human being is most deeply incarnated and properly so, later on he is often just as deeply involved in the body but then not to the advantage of his spirit.

In the thirties we conquer a piece of the earth in order to live and work on it. Sometimes now a first serious apocalyptic tone can be heard through the din of life at full swing. It reminds us that here on the earth there is no secure resting place. These apocalyptic notes can be heard in ancient history in the life story of King Jehoshaphat. Certain scenes reveal a wisdom that can be summed up in three words: 'I', sacrifice, and judgment.

When the 'I' of the human being learns in the thirties to enter fully into his will and use it as his most important tool, then it must simultaneously learn to make voluntary sacrifices. In the twenties we take from the world; through watching, hearing, feeling, learning and the proper exercise of the intellect we are absorbing and enriching ourselves; receiving, we enjoy the world. In the thirties we find a new pleasure in life — we discover the joy of *action,* the satisfaction to be found in taking our practical abilities in hand. If the will now merely collects, gathering and drawing to itself the physical world in the form of physical objects or legal documents, then we can conclude perhaps that skillfulness is at work, but the question remains open as to the goodness. The acquiring man is, in himself, not yet good, sometimes he is evil.

Property originates in rights and the law. And the law

is limited power. To begin with, property is morally neutral; its employment, however, and often the unintended effects of its very existence place the owner in a position to decide between good and evil. The words which Conrad Ferdinand Meyer has the Caliph Harun al Rashid hear from his youngest son apply on a minor scale to anyone who is an owner: 'You are all-powerful over innumerable fates here on earth — that is robbery of your brothers — and you will be judged.' Then the son disappears into the mass of the people, sacrificing himself and atoning for the existential guilt of the ruler, who from now on knows that his most beloved son is unrecognized in the multitude. His last words are: 'Look down on the many unknown, who serve you, one of them blesses you from morning until evening.'

2.18 Sacrifice

Rights and the law, property, and a beginning in the exercise of power play an important role in the thirties. The earthly experience of the 'I', the sense of ego, is based, at least to begin with, thereupon. The creation of this self-awareness cannot be avoided. Its destruction, to which materialistic socialism inclines, can easily lead to the destruction of the human soul itself. But neither will the development of this sense of self alone suffice for the salvation of mankind. It must always be perfected, complemented by sacrifice and feel itself under the judgment of God.

Standing before us as a reminder and exhortation are the ages of thirty and thirty-three in the life of Jesus: at thirty years, he gave up all the personal elements in his life when the divine ego, the 'I' of God, began its work in him; at thirty-three, he gave up life itself. In him the three stages of 'I', sacrifice, and judgment were fulfilled with extreme force, brevity and purity. Mankind and also the individual are allowed more time. At first the need to sacrifice stands before the person of thirty as a quiet summons; to begin with, he is not compelled. The necessity to go beyond the limits of one's own person usually comes only seven years later. Should the great and wise sacrifice somehow be fitted in at thirty-three years, then his life finds its final determination in a felicitous way. Then a glow of the life of Jesus surrounds it. The power of Christ now enters — far beyond the level of devout feelings — into the very will of the person. The positive power of 'predestination' from the being of Christ begins anew to form and shape the *Zeitgestalt,* the biography of this individual life. A shimmer of life eternal becomes visible in a transitory, earthly lifetime. St Augustine (AD 354 – 430) had achieved a leading position in the Roman Empire by this time in his life. After complete renunciation of that worldliness in his thirty-third year, there fell to him a leading position in humanity, which has now lasted over fifteen centuries.

At least by the thirty-fifth year, a Christian should understand that life represents more than an opportunity to create a personal kingdom. It also requires a sacrifice if it is to be inwardly fruitful. More accurately said, for a healthy life of soul and for spiritual fruitfulness, the proper sacrifice must occur. The possibility for sacrifice usually comes in the form of an urgent need or great problem which we perceive in the world around us. We must then recognize this need and grasp the opportunity.

2.19 The second moon node

At the age of thirty-seven, with the second moon node, we are forced to sacrifice. The first node partially frees the soul from its body; the second frees it from its human surroundings. However, this particular liberation is usually experienced as an expulsion. At this age, Fichte had to leave Jena, where he had been happier and able to work harder than ever again was possible. Goethe was clever enough at this critical age to escape to Italy. Returning, he found himself alienated from his old circle of friends. The series of moon nodes in a lifetime can reveal similar experiences. The enlightenment that is characteristic of the first one can return in a different form for the second or may be noticed for the first time. A good example of this is presented by the vision of Frederick the Great's last physician, the Swiss Johann Georg Zimmermann, who was born on October 8, 1728 and who on the morning of November 5, 1765 wrote:

> If an enemy of all superstition, of all 'omens', presagings, apparitions and dreams says he will relate to you the story of a dream, a dream that is not an invention, your attention [may] be awakened.
>
> [In his dream I wanted] to go into a house unknown to me. I was told: in this moment your long-since deceased wife (who, thank God, is alive and healthy) has gone into this house with another person who has also long since been dead ... I went inside and immediately opened the first door. There I saw my wife ... but as it appeared to me, entirely made up of light clouds ... [I asked]: 'Tell me above all, how are you doing in this unknown land of immortality ...'
>
> 'I am learning things,' she answered, 'that no human being would ever have supposed. I see the past clearly in all its causes and effects; every present moment is a

72

sea of ideas for me. Only the future is a little opaque for me . . . but altogether I know everything that went on in the hearts of the people I knew in the world . . . I even know all that you are now thinking, even though you may not tell me . . .'

'You are explaining to me what the greatest spirit among mortals never saw . . . let me write it down . . .' I sat down to write and suddenly awakened . . . But I could not remember the great, new and future-encompassing ideas. The following morning I wrote with the firm resolution that I would remain as faithful to the truth in this tale as if my blessedness depended upon it; and God knows that I have so remained.

The second moon node, with its generally occurring social expulsion, can also reveal the characteristic danger of the third moon node, which is the expulsion from the world of earth altogether, death. With Zimmermann, this danger was only indicated by the form of the vision: a conversation with a dead person. An expert in the field of literature and the fine arts was immediately able to think of seventeen people who died in the year of their second moon node. The series begins with Raphael, van Gogh and Byron.

2.20 The forties

Forty years is the age at which a human being should have achieved the goals he set for himself in life. The professor who guided my doctoral work told me when I was twenty-five: 'You must be a full professor by age forty at the latest.' The Greeks set the peak of human development, of the unfolding of the human soul, the acme, at forty years. This peak, representing the full blossoming of abilities, is climbed today only with conscious effort.

There appears to be a higher, spiritual law of biography, according to which great teachers of mankind only begin to work at the age of forty. We do not find Jesus and Elisha among them because the significance of their deeds and sufferings far outweighed that of their teachings. Then too, Gautama Buddha began teaching in his thirty-sixth year. But Plato, Paul, Plotinus and Steiner, among many others, first began with their own teaching at forty years of age; Moses needed twice forty years.

In the forties, a woman sees how her children are growing up. With children around, we are able to re-experience the stages of our own growth. In this way, our souls are kept fresh. A mother in her forties can accompany her children through the years in which they become independent. Ideally she will not have to ask what life might still hold for her. For life still has much to bring. In old China the matrons then came to power in their extended families. The man in his forties now becomes able to coordinate the work of his younger colleagues. He feels satisfaction when their abilities unfold in a fruitful fashion and therefore arranges everything so that each one finds his proper field of work. In short: he can now become the boss.

In the forties temptations also increase. Of the three irresistible forces, sex, money and power, the third now acquires a decisive edge in the competition for our attentions. Goethe had Faust live with the three forces in sequence. Only in old age did Faust fall prey to power, with its servant violence, when he allowed Philemon and Baucis, the old couple with the church on the dunes, to be quickly done away with in helping the evil Kaiser to victory; and when, as the prince of the newly-won marshes of the sea, he found piracy acceptable. Until approximately his thirty-fifth year, Faust had acquired the spiritual goods of mankind as a scholar — just as others do on a smaller scale in their twenties. Then relatively late in life came earthly love with Gretchen. The elevation of this into the realm of his entire soul life he experienced with Helena, and its transformation into a spiritually redeeming force he experienced only after death. Property and power, for which other people struggle in their thirties and forties, Faust first achieved in old age. Money and power have (and not only for Faust) the diabolical advantage of not losing their attraction until death. Many men, however, assign the three irresistible forces respectively to the twenties, thirties and forties. People who succeed in the world soon recognize power as the greatest among them. It requires battle.

A human being can struggle with himself and become, as Plato says, 'stronger than himself'; we can master our lower desires and thereby transform them into higher powers. This is not a battle that can be won all at once and usually never 'once and for all'. Correspondingly, nature releases the human being only by stages from the protection she has given him in his instinctive inhibitions. For example, a beneficial constraint is to be found in the mutually-felt mild antipathy existing between boys and girls in the first years of puberty. Another one lies in the instinctive revulsion felt by young people to the exercise of power for its own sake. Man is released from his inhibitions only gradually. If he wages a poor battle against the lower forces, they will intensify in the course of the forties to a degree that can be fatal.

In Goethe's *Faust* the earth-bound seeress Erichtho says on the old battlefield where Caesar and Pompey wrestled like demigods for the globe: 'How often it has already repeated itself! . . . no one can permit another to have the kingdom; no one can grant it to him, who acquired it with force and forcefully rules. For everyone who does not know how to govern himself within, governs far too eagerly the will of his neighbor, according to his own proud disposition.' At that time (August 9, 48 BC), when Pompey lost his kingdom near Pharsalus in Thessaly, and soon thereafter his life as well, he was fifty-eight years old.

2.21 *Julius Caesar*

Julius Caesar (100–44 BC) is more important for us because his life adhered almost exactly to the laws of biographical development. He received his training as an officer between the ages of nineteen and twenty-one. Between twenty-four and twenty-seven he studied with the great philosopher and historian Posidonius (135–51 BC) on the island of Rhodes. His thirties he dedicated, with varying success, to a striving for the first position in Rome. In doing so, his hidden involvement with the conspiracy of Catiline made his thirty-seventh year a very dangerous one. During the seven-year period between forty-two and forty-nine, he conquered Gaul, practically making it into his own possession. At fifty-one years he crossed the Rubicon and in yearly campaigns subjugated all the provinces of the Roman Empire. He simultaneously promoted the cultural life of the Empire through a farsighted legislative program stressing freedom. At fifty-six, as he stood poised to reach for the crown of Rome and, like his model Alexander the Great, begin a war against the Parthians, he fell by the daggers of his murderers.

As the rule would have it, Julius Caesar's twenties were devoted to the development of the mind, his thirties to working within the framework of the existing society, and the forties to establishing his own kingdom. The sole meaning of Julius Caesar's fifties was centered in his work as a lawmaker. His mistake was to extend the task proper to the forties into his fifties and so his unlimited desire to conquer led to downfall. At this point, taking a look at a biography that broke the rules may be rewarding. Alexander (356–323 BC) came to power in Macedonia at twenty years of age. After a twelve-year campaign leading to lordship over half the world, he died aged thirty-three in Babylon. His twenties, which others use to conquer the world in ideas, forced him to immediate deeds of world conquest. These accomplishments were as ingenious as they were magnificent and went beyond almost anything ever achieved in the world of men. A metamorphosis of this life-style in the thirties, that is, in the years otherwise reserved for such tasks, appears to have been impossible. From the point of view of the human *Zeitgestalt*, Alexander's early death was unavoidable.

2.22 *Augustus Caesar*

At nineteen years of age, after Julius Caesar's death, Octavianus Augustus (63 BC – AD 14) began fighting for his inheritance. At thirty-three he concluded this battle with the sea-victory near Actium over Mark Antony, followed by his entrance into Egyptian Alexandria on August 1, 30 BC. The long years of battle during his twenties were not pursued in the fashion of his predecessor Alexander, the transformer of the world. Rather, he fought as the executor of Julius Caesar's estate, doing only what many before him had long recognized as necessary and desirable. Thereafter he permitted as many official functions as possible to be discharged by others, in the fashion of the old republican civil service. In this way, the ruler who was so sickly at the beginning of his career lived to be seventy-seven years old, thereby creating a very successful *Zeitgestalt*.

2.23 Fichte

An example of great achievement in the middle years of life, which is also an exception to the rule, is found in the great German philosopher Johann Gottlieb Fichte (1762–1814). In Fichte's twenties, he was attached to the thinking of Spinoza, a system which well occupied his intellect, but did not really satisfy his still hidden spirit; it did not stir his soul. As a result, Fichte's inner and outer progress during this time remained meagre. At twenty-nine, he found his liberation through Kant. Fichte soon outgrew Kant and became a thinker of his own school. While most people seek confirmation during their thirties in outward-directed activities, Fichte, though also developing his will at this time, sent it into new ideas of the greatest significance. He used his thinking to reach out and understand the very existence of the world from a new, sustaining point, which he characterized with a word meant to convey a suprapersonal reality, the 'I', the ego. Mankind had never before experienced reality being carried and thought in a mind permeated by a will so pure and so powerful as Fichte's. The appearance of this phenomenon was no doubt helped by the artifice of destiny allowing the thinker to be awakened only at the beginning of his thirties.

Yet Johann Wolfgang Goethe's life of eighty-three years offers the greatest example of a full and perfected biography in tune with the laws of the human *Zeitge-*

stalt. Goethe's life could, all by itself, serve as a guide for a new science of biography. But such a study would require an entire book; we have taken the shorter biblical path.

2.24 Mars and the planets

Returning to the forties, we again consider the life of the great Gaius Julius Caesar, who at this age found his own unique style and work in life. It would be useless to try and conceal the fact that Mars governs life in the forties. In the main, the forties lead people to the power that has been allotted them in this life. For the sake of wisdom and human love, however, Mars would then like to be overcome through the power of renunciation. If this can be achieved, then he gives us the power to affect large numbers of people through the power of the word and thereby work for the good. The word works powerfully and to good effect when renunciation lies hidden within it.

What does the name of the planet Mars have to do with biography? In Goethe's novel, *Wilhelm Meister's Travels*, Wilhelm Meister meets a holy woman by the name of Makarie. She experiences in full consciousness what every human being experiences unconsciously, step by step, from birth to death. Of her is said:

> Makarie is related to our solar system in a way which one hardly dares to say. In the spirit, in the soul, in the power of imagination she protects, she not only sees it, but rather she comprises a part of the same; she sees herself pulled along in those heavenly circles; but in an entirely different way; she wanders since her childhood around the sun and, indeed, as has now been discovered, in a spiral constantly more and more distant from the middle point and circling toward the outward regions.

In her old age, her statements reveal

> that she, long since over the orbit of Mars, now is approaching the orbit of Jupiter . . . [Later] it was concluded that she was seeing it from the side and was really about to go beyond this orbit and strive toward Saturn in the limitless space. There no power of imagination could follow her; but we hope that such an entelechy would not entirely remove itself from our solar system at death, but, when she has come to the limits of the same, would wish to return in order to again work into earthly life and dispense charity for the benefit of our descendants.

2.25 *Turning the corner at forty-nine*

At seven times seven years of age, the body's creative life-forces leave the woman. *The Man of Fifty Years* (as Goethe titled his novel characterizing this age) likes to immerse himself in an opposite notion. As a matter of fact, an inclination toward men of fifty often awakens in young girls beginning around the age of seventeen. However, fifty years is not the age for a possible bridegroom but rather the age of their fathers and should so remain. The family and friends immediately surrounding these girls are called upon silently to protect them from this tendency; there is no real happiness or future in such unions. In truth, the man in his fifties must work at achieving what the woman does out of her own nature. Life shows this to be a general law: the man must exert conscious effort to achieve what the woman usually does out of her own nature.

At fifty years of age (originally at sixty), generals and other men in ancient Rome who had served their country in the highest capacities became mature enough to be Senators. Their generally very active lives were, as such, now ended; for them personally, money, power and honor were already attained and a suprapersonal perspective had matured them for a new service. Their farsightedness and dignity enabled the Senate to appear as an assembly comprised of kings; Jupiter now ruled their souls. Today also, even in modest affairs, it is advisable to entrust wealth that is to be administered for the benefit of many, to the care of people over fifty years of age, if extraordinary undertakings are not required.

2.26 *The sphere of death*

Searching in old church records for the generation of our great-grandfathers, and even earlier, reveals the old tradition of men dying aged fifty-six. Of course there were many other cases, but as far as I have been able to check, it seems to have been a very common custom for an ordinary man, who had energetically taken hold of life as it came to meet him from outside, but who had not made any particularly noticeable efforts in the soul realm to master it from within, contracted the required case of pneumonia and died thereof. The eighth seven-year period was then completed and the third moon node (fifty-five years, nine months and twelve days) had entered the field. Shortly before Goethe's third moon node he lost his good friend Schiller and found himself in a health crisis.

Also in our time when men can expect to live longer, these years can be a time of crisis. Heart attacks that prove to be fatal are a frequent occurrence around this time. The rule that in every seven-year period we have something unique to learn shows itself here too; but if at this junction we do not take up the lesson to be learned, then life itself tends to end. Perfection is not required or expected, but one has seven years to learn in and no longer. The transition into the fifties is usually a very difficult one for lively active people.

The Saturn time of our lives then begins. Here judgment is passed on us. Happy is he who can love the judgment because his life-long striving for the good has led him to absorb the standards of the court into his very own being. Then Saturn does not take anything from him that he cannot let go. Much rather does life now acquire a new depth and quality of truth. Happy is he who is still permitted to work. He will probably remain a person of value to many people and for a long time. Saturn leads those who affirm his judgment to their hidden spiritual being. The unreconciled nature of this planet is carried in the soul of the old harp player described by Goethe in *Wilhelm Meister*. The harpist sings:

> Who never ate his bread with tears
> Who never the care-filled nights
> Spent sitting on his bed crying
> He knows you not, you heavenly powers.
> You lead us into life
> You make the poor indebted
> Then you leave him to the pain;
> For on earth all debts are revenged.

2.27 Old age

The remaining years of life follow the view of Goethe according to which in youth we are idealists, in the middle of life we are realists and in old age we become mystics. Lacking experience myself I must now borrow from the description of a senior friend who is over eighty years of age. His words to me were somewhat as follows:

> What all too many men first experience when they retire at age sixty-five is generally known. Anyone who has clung to the old ways of work, who was not able to alter his attitude toward work must stumble over this threshold; he stumbles very easily into death. But if he has managed to change his ways, at least by the beginning of the sixties and has found a new joy in work, then he will make it over the threshold of sixty-three to sixty-five. But he may then find an even more difficult step in the seventies. It is especially likely that a pastor would notice this for he is probably still permitted to do the same work as in years past. For this reason he is perhaps less well prepared for the threshold of the seventies than a successful graduate of the previous test.
>
> Having passed this threshold I have observed the following: Over seventy and even more so over seventy-two I could no longer do what had been long planned; I was no longer able to hold myself to a schedule as I had previously. If now in old age I still attempt to adhere to a schedule, either I fall from a bicycle [this friend lived in Holland] or something similar happens to me. I simply get out of bed on the wrong side in the morning. Now I must listen every morning and simply try to perceive anew what exactly must happen that day.
>
> Then, once this has been discovered, things usually work out very well — at least, to the extent that I begin immediately. Work schedules for weeks ahead or even years ahead such as I created for myself in the past can no longer exist for me. I live, not in years of grace as this time of life is often called but rather in days of grace. I would say that the book of my life is completely filled. Everything is now to be found written within just as it was entered; there can be no more corrections. However, loose supplementary pages are permitted; and they are, when properly written, also enjoyable. I feel that they will be added to my life, spiritually added.

3 The Gifts of the Hierarchies

3.1 The resurrection as goal

We observed that the Greeks prized man's form in space while Israel, on the other hand, had a special understanding for man's *Zeitgestalt*. This understanding first applied to the history of the nation, then to mankind's origin and destiny which are expressed in the biblical myths. The general contours of mankind's history are made clear in the beginning of Genesis and also in the apocalyptic books which appeared during the centuries around Christ's birth. It was left to Christianity, however, to achieve an understanding of the *Zeitgestalt* of the single individual. In his speech on the Areopagus in Athens (Acts 17:22), Paul first spoke to the Greeks concerning the statues he saw upon entering the town. In so doing, he was touching on mankind's common shape in space. Then, in mentioning the day of the last judgment, he is drawing to his hearers' attention the *Zeitgestalt* of all mankind. Finally, he spoke of the renewal of the image of God through the resurrection of Christ. In the Acts of the Apostles, Luke has Paul begin as follows (17:23–24):

> For as I passed along [through your city] . . . I found also an altar with this inscription, 'To an unknown god.' What therefore you worship as unknown, this I proclaim to you. The God who made the world and everything in it, being Lord of heaven and earth . . . And he made from one every nation of men . . . As even some of your poets have said, 'For we are indeed his offspring' . . . He has fixed a day on which he will judge the world in righteousness by a man whom he has

84

> appointed, and of this he has given assurance to all men
> by raising him from the dead.

Luke then closes the address: 'So Paul went out from among them. But some men joined him and believed, among them Dionysius the Areopagite.'

For Paul, Christianity stands or falls with the resurrection of Jesus (1Cor.15). To understand the resurrection he sees it in connection with the Creation and the Fall. That this is in accordance with scripture is shown by the variations of God's first saying concerning man. The Godhead had spoken: 'Let us make man in our own image, after our likeness' (Gen.1:26). Then Eve heard the following concerning God's 'image and likeness' from the direction of the earth, that is, out of the mouth of the serpent: 'Did God say, "you shall not eat of any tree in the garden?" ... For God knows that when you eat of it your eyes will be opened, and you will be like God, knowing good and evil.' (Gen.3:1,5).

With these two scenes in mind, Paul writes in his Letter to the Philippians (2:5–10):

> Have this mind among yourselves, which is yours in Christ Jesus, who, though he was in the form of God, did not count equality with God a thing to be grasped, but emptied himself, taking the form of a servant, being born in the likeness of men. And being found in human form he humbled himself and became obedient unto death, even death on a cross. Therefore, God has highly exalted him and bestowed on him the name which is above every name, that at the name of Jesus every knee should bow, in heaven and on earth and under the earth.

Paul also writes, in Colossians (1:12–18):

> ... giving thanks to the Father ... He has delivered us from the dominion of darkness and transferred us to the kingdom of his beloved Son, in whom we have redemption, the forgiveness of sins.

He is the image of the invisible God, the first-born of all creation; for in him all things were created, in heaven and on earth, visible and invisible whether thrones or dominions or principalities or authorities — all things were created through him and for him ... He is the head of the body, the church; he is the beginning, the first-born from the dead, that in everything he might be pre-eminent.

The resurrection happened to Jesus Christ and has thereby become a fact for the world. Because it stands entirely alone, at first the world cannot understand it; for understanding and thinking mean comparing. The resurrection of Christ is incomparable, unless one places it next to the creation of man as described in the Bible; and that is exactly what Paul does in his First Letter to the Corinthians (15:21–22).

For us human beings, the resurrection represents a goal. Together with the creation of the new world, which in the book of Revelation is called the new Jerusalem, it is the final goal. Even the simplest biography is dependent upon the particular goals which are carried in a man's soul; how much more the final goal of mankind leaves its imprint on our lives.

Paul unites the resurrection with a *pleroma* of hierarchical angelic beings. The Hebrew word for God, who created heaven and earth, and who spoke his first words concerning man in Genesis (1:26), is a noun in the plural, that is, he spoke in the company of high spiritual beings. Even more does the resurrection of Jesus involve a fullness of heavenly hierarchies.

The Pauline angelology is not simple and for the world view of contemporary man it can seem very strange. To enter into it, despite this, is to be confronted immediately with an even greater problem: Paul takes into consideration not only the good angels of the various orders, but also the evil forces within the hierarchies. One quotation from the Letter to the Ephesians illustrates what could also be found in many other passages: 'Put on the whole armour of God, that you may be able to stand against the wiles of the devil. For we are not contending against flesh and blood, but against the principalities [*archaí*], against the powers [*exousíai*], against the world rulers of this present darkness, against the spiritual hosts of wickedness in the heavenly places.' (Eph.6:11–12.) The eighteenth century erased all consciousness of the devil from the European mind. Actually, any awareness whatsoever of evil spiritual forces was eliminated. Logically enough, the nineteenth century then proceeded to eliminate any awareness of good angelic forces. However, if we are to strive for a spiritual and Christian conception of the world, then we must again learn to think of and deal with all of the spiritual beings mentioned in the Bible, the bad as well as the good.

Just as the ten first sayings of God in Genesis concerning man served us in the first of these chapters, so will the nine hierarchies of angels serve us now as a guiding thread. Mankind is destined one day to form a tenth hierarchy under these nine. The hierarchies will then speak as God spoke at the end of the Creation: 'man has become like one of us . . .' (Gen.3:22).

In order better to understand, we are placing the science of biography in the light of creation and in the light of the resurrection. As a third source of light, we also have the teaching of the hierarchies, who, according to Paul, are intimately related to the resurrection of Christ. From the origin and the goal of man we take the measure for his life.

3.2 *The spiritual kingdoms above man*

The Old Testament first gives us a complete picture of the hierarchies in Jacob's dream at Bethel:

> And he dreamed that there was a ladder set up on the earth, and the top of it reached to heaven; and behold, the angels of God were ascending and descending on it! And behold, the LORD stood above it and said, 'I am the LORD, the God of Abraham your father and the God of Isaac; the land on which you lie I will give to you and your descendants ... I am with you and will keep you wherever you go, and will bring you back to this land' (Gen.28:12–15).

The greatest vision of the hierarchies in the Bible appeared to Isaiah in the Temple at Jerusalem when he was called to be a prophet:

> In the year that King Uzziah died, I saw the LORD sitting upon a throne, high and lifted up; and his train filled the temple. Above him stood the seraphim; each had six wings: with two he covered his face, and with two he covered his feet, and with two he flew. And one called to another and said:
>
> 'Holy, holy, holy is the LORD of [heavenly] hosts;
> the whole earth is full of his glory.'
>
> And the foundations of the thresholds shook at the voice of him who called, and the house was filled with smoke. And I said: 'Woe me! For I am lost; for I am a man of unclean lips ... for my eyes have seen the King, the LORD of hosts' (Isa.6:1–5).

The first name of one of these holy orders we hear already in connection with Adam: 'the LORD sent him forth from the garden of Eden, to till the ground [*adamah*] from which he was taken. He drove out the man; and at the east of the garden of Eden he placed the cherubim, and a flaming sword ...' (Gen.3:23f).

The angelic name most frequently heard in the Old Testament is 'the angel of the LORD'; the book of Daniel also speaks of Gabriel and Michael. The evangelists continue using these names in the birth accounts and in the reports of the resurrection, also at the temptation and in Luke's description of Christ in Gethsemane. Jesus himself speaks of the 'holy angels' in the parables of the last days, and almost always when he mentions the second coming of the Son of Man (Matt.16:27, and so on). It is only in Paul's letters that we first read about the multiplicity and the names of the choirs of angels. However, Paul does not present us with a well-organized unified teaching. There are only fragments of such a doctrine; fragments, to be sure, which are unmatched in their magnificence.

In ancient times we already find Isaiah's vision in the temple inserted into the Christian communion service between the Offering and the Transubstantiation; the names of the orders of the angels were spoken. In the communion service of The Christian Community, the Act of Consecration of Man, this invocation is heard at Christmas time.

Sometime around AD 500 the orders of the angels were written down for the first time in summarized fashion. The originator is given as Dionysius, whom Paul won over as a disciple through his address on the Areopagus (Acts 17:34). In Paris, around the middle of the ninth century, John Scotus Erigena translated these writings into Latin. From then on, the influence they exerted on the theology and mysticism of the Middle Ages was second only to that exerted by the Gospels. These writings on the hierarchies abide by teachings given by Paul; they are, however, also penetrated through and through by the spirit of Plato and his

disciples Plotinus and Proclus. The Platonists understood evil only as weakness and as the absence of the
good; in the Good alone Being itself was grounded. But
they overlooked something. In the course of world evolution, where Being becomes finite existence, it is possible for an evil being to give itself an anti-divine form
and then use it, circumstances permitting, powerfully to
influence other beings. Therefore, Dionysius the Areopagite, as a Platonist, was, unlike Paul, not at all inter-
ested in evil powers. His teaching thereby lost the drama
of life. For him, the higher hierarchies became merely
intensifications of the lower hierarchies. A reader of
these writings almost has the impression that Dionysius's enumeration of the angelic orders, although
ninefold, actually represents a simplification of the
manifold picture conveyed by Paul's letters.

In spite of that, we shall use the ninefold enumeration; it can conveniently be surveyed. But we shall try
to bring back to it some of the old life that it had for
Paul. We shall also make use of the manifold descriptions by Rudolf Steiner which still further enliven this
teaching of the hierarchies, which the theology of the
twentieth century has otherwise lost entirely. Anyone
today who wants to acquire a vital, living doctrine of
the angels must inevitably turn to Paul, Dionysius the
Areopagite and Rudolf Steiner as sources. In the context
of this book, it would not be appropriate to quote at
length. For this reason you, as a friendly reader, should
clearly hold the view that the author is speaking from
learned knowledge and in no way out of his own personal clairvoyance. He would like to clear himself at
the outset of any suspicion of arrogance, to which,
because of the high and noble character of their subject,
theologians are so often exposed. We now examine a

brief description of the hierarchies, after which our glance will return to earth, where we shall remain, considering only that which can be experienced on the earth.

According to Dionysius, the names of the heavenly orders are: angeloi, archangeloi, archai, exousiai, dynameis, kyriotetes, thronoi, cherubim and seraphim. Seven of these names are Greek, the last two Hebrew in the plural. In English they are called: angels, archangels, principalities, powers, virtues, dominions, thrones, cherubim and seraphim. The Hebrew names were taken over by Christendom without questioning the content of the words. In the Act of Consecration of Man, in the great Christmas invocation to the Father, they are called: angels, archangels, archai, revealers, world powers, world guides, thrones, cherubim and seraphim. Some of these names were created by Rudolf Steiner. He described them in his lectures in many ways. In particular he characterized the archai as spirits of time and as spirits of personality, the exousiai as spirits of form, the dynameis as the spirits of movement, the kyriotetes as the spirits of wisdom, the thrones as the spirits of will, the cherubim as the spirits of the harmonies, and the seraphim as the spirits of love.

3.3 The workings of the hierarchies

With their power, the seraphim hold the spiritual and therefore the physical cosmos together. Their being consists of spiritual fire and they live in perfect devotion to the threefold Godhead above them.

The cherubim give order to the universe with their radiant wisdom.

The thrones send courage and will into the

nothingness of space, which they first create. Time also comes into existence through their ongoing activity. Our solar system also comes into being and continues to exist through the thrones' continually sacrificing their very being into the world.

The kyriotetes or world guides are filled with wonder as they behold the sacrifice of the thrones. In accordance with this beholding wonder they organize the substance that has gone forth from the thrones into the system of the sun and the planets. Alone, the kyriotetes cannot create existence, but they can awaken the life therein. For the beings beneath them, they send out a spiritual light in which truth, wisdom and good are still undifferentiated. They still stand far above the possibility of evil. Plato was able, in his most sublime ideas, to reflect something of these beings.

The dynameis or world powers regulate the circling of the planets and all the movements governed thereby. Their inner life is characterized by a productive resignation or submission to world destiny. In human souls today, their work is becoming increasingly important and more and more requires the active participation of human beings if their task is to be accomplished. On this subject, I will have more to say later.

From the dynameis downward through the hierarchies, we must also reckon with workings and activities which require courage on our part merely to imagine. Otherwise, we remain with Dionysius in that form of Neoplatonism which painted light on light and in so doing lost sight of the wills involved, of the battle of power among spiritual beings, and of the gravity of the opposition between good and evil. Dionysius appears to have only known angels who exerted a powerful, good and ennobling effect on man. Paul, however, also speaks of hierarchical beings who exert an evil influence. He does this only for the dynameis and the beings below them; unless he means even greater beings than these with the expressions 'high thing' (2Cor.10:5 'proud obstacle' in RSV) and 'depth' (Eph.3:18), which he also sometimes uses. To the Romans (8:38–39) he writes: 'For I am sure that neither death, nor life, nor angels, nor principalities, nor things present, nor things to come, nor powers, nor *height*, nor *depth*, nor anything else in all creation, will be able to separate us from the love of God in Christ Jesus our Lord.' In this passage, 'things present' and 'things to come' allude to the archai as spirits of time. However, it is not so clear that 'height' and 'depth' refer in the same way to the dynameis; it is merely probable, not certain.

The exousiai or revealers create the clear forms of the solar system. They do this with the planets in their entirety and on a smaller scale with all solid matter as much as possible. They create the crystals and are altogether the originators of this world of things, which contains a great multiplicity constructed from a very small number of elements or aggregate states. If we consider all the possible forms and shapes of fluid and air-flow with vortices, and so on, in addition to the solid creations, then we are thinking of the new and multiplex formed plane of existence, for the creation of which the exousiai are responsible. Together with the dynameis, the exousiai bring about the spin of the earth; that is, the rhythm of day and night; and this, along with their working in the external and spiritual light, is the most important precondition for our consciousness of ourselves as selves, that is, for the development of the spiritual kernel of the human being known as the 'ego' or 'I'. This consciousness is, to begin with, a consciousness of things. The exousiai are themselves the fathers of our egos. They have made our bodies to stand upright and have given us the countenance in which God seeks his image. In our souls, the exousiai create clear and definite concepts. Mathematics and logic are their work.

Among all the other hierarchies, these 'revealers' sat in the front row of the secret council in which God spoke 'Let us make man in our image, after our likeness' (Gen.1:26). At that time, God's thought concerning dry land (Gen.1:9) already existed; man then became the most perfect being to walk upon it. This is related to the fact that in the entire pattern of creation in six days the first three days correspond to the second three; here the third day saw the creation of land, while on the sixth man was created.

The archai or principalities govern the succession of great epochs of man's cultural development; for example, the Old Egyptian, the Greek, the Middle Ages and the modern era. For this reason, Steiner named them spirits of time.

They have no influence on the physical body of the human being. The powers of the three lower orders of angels do not reach that far. A lower group among the archai influences large civilizations existing simultaneously, yet in disparate parts of the earth, such as in Eastern Asia or in North America. The archai work on the half-conscious will and influence those general actions of men which proceed from the realm of habit. In this way, they create the social order and the occupations and professions of an age. Occupation and social position work to give the human soul the character which makes it into a personality on earth. The 'person' behind this personality is not the spiritual kernel of the human being; it is rather the garment, so to speak, that lies closest to him.

It is perhaps easiest for us to see among the ranks of the archai those spiritual workings that strengthen the effects of evil among men upon the earth. This aspect of the hierarchies, at least of the archai, must now be discussed to guard against the illusion that wherever we notice superhuman forces among us we are necessarily reckoning with truth and goodness. The archai not only influence the common habits of a country or civilization, they also involve themselves in widespread opinions, the so-called 'public opinion'. The more prejudice it contains and the more it is guided by lies and half-truths, the more the evil archai are involved. Our century has seen entire peoples made the target of slander in this way. Other archai cultivate the various races of mankind — as if inadequately imitating the exousiai, who created the general and specific bodily forms of humanity. Others closely related to these stimulate passions of the blood and also make a person's thoughts passionate, egotistically bound up with a single group, or simply all too personal. The source of black magic is to be found in even more evil archai, who have the goal of sending their will, so to speak, through unguarded doors into the souls of their victims; hypnosis is the beginning of this. From now on, we shall consider only those effects of the orders of the angels which are good and life-sustaining. In particular, we shall examine the angelic forces which work into our lives in a regular fashion.

The archangels work into the feelings of man. They cause entire populations to have common sentiments and feelings. The mightiest among them cultivate and directly influence languages — others are the leaders of peoples and nations. Angels lead individuals to that which the person can experience through his senses. The physical environment creates the framework and the general conditions for an individual destiny. So every angel has the thread of destiny for one human being in his hand. There are also those who, in an entirely good sense, act as if they were archangels in leading the greater political figures.

We have now sufficient ideas and notions concerning the work of the ranks of angels to understand the life of a human being from the other side, so to speak, where there is no matter which our physical senses can perceive.

3.4 How the angels work in our lives

Our angel represents us before God. Therefore, we often call him 'God' in our prayers. Every human being has his angel whose task it is to lead him through life. This path begins with a joint preview of the upcoming life on earth. The writer of the Psalms says (Ps.139:16):

> Thy eyes beheld my unformed substance;
> in thy book were written, every one of them,
> the days that were formed for me,
> when as yet there were none of them.

Not only does mankind as a whole have a book of life, as is described in the twentieth chapter of the Book of Revelation, but every human being has a book containing a heavenly plan for his life. There are Chinese ink drawings which make clear everything they have to say with only two or three strokes; the book of life for any individual before he is born is similar. If all goes well, this sketch will be a fully completed painting after seventy years.

After this preview, the soul begins to descend into the body, which is slowly being formed within the womb of the mother. Then it goes to sleep. During this time, the embryo is imbued with and shaped by certain forces. These are the forces from which the human being has been woven according to the hidden counsel taken by God with the higher hierarchies since ancient times. After birth, and then only step by step with the stages of growth, the soul awakens to its earthly life within the body.

The angel protects the time of sleeping and dreamy awakening — the parents of the child have the task of helping during this process. In concert with the mighty powers of creation from much higher hierarchies, the angel exerts an influence not only on the parents, but also on the wider circle of people around the child. One sometimes has the impression that many unborn children possess the power to create for themselves a further sheath, or 'housing' beyond the physical body, for example an apartment for the family. Only when they are born are they really in need of help. Now the angel truly becomes a guardian angel, without which the child would not escape the dangers of its environment. The angel does this work until the fourteenth year — approximately until confirmation.

When, around the time of confirmation, the angel releases the child, he declares that the deeds of that human being shall from then on be considered as his own. Parents handle children in much the same fashion; if a child does something mischievous or dangerous, then we discuss it with him on the same day until he understands it as much as he is able. Afterwards, the matter must drop out of sight for the child. When he awakes in the morning, his deeds do not wake with him. If it were otherwise, it would be injurious for him psychologically or even physically. But after confirmation, the young person begins to write his own book of destiny. From now on, there also apply to him the words which are spoken for the dead in the Book of Revelation, 'for their deeds follow them!' (14:13).

In special 'emergency cases' the angel continues working as protector. Remembering many destinies known by me personally, I would dare to say: the more seriously someone takes himself in hand, the more seriously he works on his thoughts and feelings, all the more decisively will his outer destiny be spared from catastrophes affecting large masses such as are found in wartime. It is even more astounding to see how often, even in middle age, such people are saved from life-threatening situations.

Aside from such special cases, the angel proceeds more and more to 'take a vacation' from his charge in stages running parallel with the seven-year rhythm. One could imagine that the angel of an adult departs for a restful holiday and, behaving like a demanding relative, for a time he has the means for his support sent to him. His charge picks up the bill. However, toward the end of the forties, remaining with our picture, the angel's supplies are getting scarce and he begins to approach the human being again.

As a matter of fact, the inner mood of soul of many people changes around the fiftieth year; it becomes religious once more. People in their thirties often feel that they are no longer able to feel life as deeply as they did in their twenties; life itself does not seem to provide them with as much enriching experience. Unless something other than alcohol and television are used to fight against this sense of loss, the fifties will see an even worse paralysis of the soul. According to Goethe, we become idealists in youth, realists in the years of active will, and mystics in old age. Both our own efforts and those of our angel are necessary if we are indeed to become mystics; it doesn't happen by itself. If no deepening of the soul life occurs, then the soul becomes distorted and slowly becomes barren. In bygone years, pedantry, avarice and a mania for complaining often began to spread through the soul at this age. More often today, we see people living a lie against age. Fortunately, in Europe one still notices how ridiculous an older person becomes when he attempts to remain young in the fashion of his younger years. The feeling for this absurdity has almost entirely vanished in America.

Where our soul has grown together with our body, we must simply acknowledge our age. Only on a higher level of the soul can we remain young without injury: at this level we should even become childlike; precisely this enables us to become mystical in the good sense intended by Goethe. When grandmothers tell their grandchildren fairy tales in such a way that the wisdom in them can be sensed, then they are becoming childlike in the best sense of the word. Anyone who follows the fairy tale hour on radio or television will know that this cannot be achieved with childish mannerisms.

The angels need our new inner childlikeness. The images of spiritual truth such as are found, for example, in genuine fairy tales, religious ritual, and accurate thoughts concerning conditions in heaven, they take from our souls at night when we sleep. With such pictures, they can maintain contact with and cultivate the soul life of their charges. Every night angels and archangels look into our souls. But it is not worth their while to look if the day has only been spent making banal, material, earth-bound entries; then they immediately slam the book shut and turn away from the person. Higher beings such as the archai and the orders above them appear to study our books of life only in their entirety and after our deaths. We shall speak of this later.

The angels also adhere to the mystery of love. Now they urgently need the higher form of it; a form which is only developed by people who are diligent and, even more, prepared to accept suffering. This kind of love grows when the angels, like mothers who remain true to their children, courageously bear our failures, disappointments and unexpected turns in life — in short, when they share both luck and misfortune — even self-inflicted guilt and inner misadventures. This is the kind of love the angels drink in and then with their presence thank us for.

Once a life has come to its end, there follows a backward look, a 'post-view', corresponding to the preview before life began. Just as the angel once showed us the sketch of our destiny, appearing like a work of art consisting of a few pen strokes, so now we see our lived life as a painting with bright colors. To be sure, this does not always entirely agree with the preliminary sketch. Sometimes the intention may have been completely botched; often parts will have become too thick or too clouded. All in all, however, we hope to be looking at a worthwhile painting.

Anyone who has the rewarding duty of holding many memorial addresses knows that the sketch of a person's life is the most ingenious part. The sketch reveals itself superficially in dry numbers and names, in statistics, which could almost all be obtained from the state records office: When and where was this person born?

Who was the mother? What was the occupation of the father? How many brothers and sisters did he have? When and where did he begin his professional life? What was his occupation? When and where did he find his spouse? How long were they together? What were the particular blows of destiny? And so forth. The names and numbers provide us with the basic spiritual framework of a biography. It is nice if one knows more. Deeds and sacrifices should be remembered. Of course, the Roman rule, 'say nothing evil about the dead', applies to all memorial addresses. But saying the truth must remain the basic principle, for without truth the deceased himself cannot be present at any service held for him. The simple facts, properly regarded, mirror the truth without the involvement of human judgment which so often errs. The facts alone usually reveal the greatness that lies hidden in almost every biography. There may be boring people, but boring biographies do not exist. In the basic framework, great wisdom can always be found, and this is the work of the angel.

3.5 *The nation and the archangel*

Every child encounters an archangel through the fact that it lives into a language and the feelings of a nation. Language is, to be sure, the stronger element; but first we examine the other. Every nation or people is led by an archangel through its common, widespread feelings about life. In the narrowest sense, this could be called the feeling of a nation. Everything that makes itself known through customs and folk songs belongs to this common soul, which the archangel strengthens and cultivates as the spirit of a people. A royal court which is widely respected and revered can serve him as an important tool for this purpose. The archangel also looks toward the schools of a country. He is responsible for the 'upkeep' of innumerable simple and decent human souls; the strongest and best feelings that they have originate in him, and because he strengthens them they will not perish. When such people appear outside the borders of their own land, they are given moral credit. Holland, England, France, Norway, Finland and Poland are such countries whose populations enjoy the undisturbed leadership of an archangel.

This no longer holds true for Germans. If a German appears outside of Germany, he is no longer afforded moral credit as a matter of course. One may well believe that he is competent in some fields after a first demonstration, but that he can be trusted and that associating with him is worth while must be proven over a longer period of time. In the end, many people may hold him in particularly high esteem, but never simply because he is a highly perfected German. By contrast, Englishmen are often valued specifically for being good Englishmen. In a similar way, before the pathological time of the Nazis, the Jews were treated by Germans as individuals lacking a protecting folkspirit above them. Today Jews and Germans are treated similarly throughout the world; one feels that there is no shielding, soul-cultivating folk-spirit hovering over them. It was different for the Germans before the First World War and quite the opposite during the nineteenth century; the common German soul and mind was still reliable. Kant was still able to say: 'one is not German by blood, but rather by the mind and soul'. And this 'mind and soul' was rich and good.

When was this lost? In 1894, Max Weber wrote in the periodical, *Christliche Welt:*

> The opposite of political education . . . announces that
> humanly lovable softening of the heart which thinks it
> can replace political ideals with ethical ones and then
> harmlessly identifies these with optimistic good-luck
> wishes . . .
>
> We must understand that the unification of Germany
> was a youthful prank, which the nation pulled off in
> the old days and should have forgone because of its
> costliness, if it was supposed to be the conclusion and
> not the starting point of German politics as a world
> power.

In no way did Weber recommend such politics in and
of themselves, but rather with the following words he
warned against using the instrument of a world power
present in Germany at that time in a vain and dilettante
way, as Wilhelm II used it; for that would lead to
general ruin. 'We shall not succeed in eliminating the
curse of having been born after Bismarck . . . unless we
understand how to become something else — forerun-
ners of something greater . . .' In his other writings also,
Max Weber proved to be a prophet of destiny for the
next sixty years. Summarizing his comments above, one
could say: Only great and noble ideas with the power
to shape and form men's minds can help lead us into
the future — not any attempt to revive nationalistic
feelings from the past. Only in the light of this spirit
will the soul blossom. This is true not only for every
single human being, but also for nations. We can boldly
ask further what was thought in heaven about the grave
and difficult German folk destiny and what was contributed to it from that direction. Rudolf Steiner said
that in 1879 the German folk spirit separated itself from
the German people. Of course, faced with this kind of
pronouncement, one feels helpless at first; usually one
must simply set it aside and let it rest quietly before

passing any judgments. However, in this case, our experience of earthly history would appear to point in the same direction.

We must now ask the further question: Can there be a renewal of the folk spirit? Following the experience of the twentieth century, every reflective person can see that this will certainly not occur with a flourish of trumpets. If at all possible, it can only be achieved through a quiet, thoughtful preparation involving heart and conscience. It can only be a path of long, arduous work which also leads to the spiritual welfare of the individual. Only a path passing through much physical and spiritual work, through readiness to suffer and through the courageous willingness to consider all genuine questions, will lead to the longed-for discovery of self. Futhermore, the path of a nation requires sacrifices to be made by every individual, which go beyond those required for personal destiny.

To all outward appearances, Germany has not gone very far on this path. The trumpets are indeed quiet, but the superficiality of which they were the voice has not lessened. Since the 1920s the radio and since the 1950s television have contributed their deleterious tones to this superficiality. Both these media exert a leveling and blunting influence on the soul, and not merely through the content of their transmissions. This situation will probably not improve in the near future. Through tranquillity, pain, great spiritual work and prayer, a new German folk spirit could perhaps be brought down to the nation from the spiritual world.

An important experience from the beginning of the century should not be forgotten. The German youth movement, the *Wandervogel*, feeling the serious spiritual condition of the nation, tried to help out. Reaching back into the past, their attempt was twofold: first, they tried to re-enliven the rich cultural history of the people by, for example, renewing old folk songs; secondly, they tried to return to nature. The movement failed, and in the end was used to evil purpose.

Remembering is only beneficial when it serves to prepare for a spiritual step forward; then it is indispensable. The step I have in mind is toward new ideas, which portray either the final goal of all of humanity or more limited ideals which are derived from the final goal and can now be made into reality. Both kinds form a part of Christianity. However, they must be thought anew, perhaps for the first time seriously, and together with all their consequences.

There is an example of this in the history of Israel: in the ninth and eighth centuries before Christ, Israel, as a people, was in a situation similar to that of Germany of the present day. At that time, it was to be decided whether or not this people could continue to exist. The larger part of the country succumbed because, even before its defeat at the hands of the Assyrians (c. 735–722 BC), it had become alienated from its true mission by worship of the pagan god of fertility, Baal. As a result, it was unable to offer any spiritual resistance under conditions of external catastrophe. The great seductress who had led them astray was Jezebel, who was first queen and then influential queen-mother in the northern kingdom of Israel during the years 875 to 842 BC. In the state of Judah in the south, the people were, to begin with, strictly Mosaically minded — they looked back at Israel's great past with Moses, David and Solomon. Yet nothing was undertaken against Jezebel's evil goals. Even the pious king Jehoshaphat, who prepared the way for her historically, did not recognize the danger she represented. He fetched her daugher, Atha-liah, to Jerusalem to be the crown-princess. Some time later she made herself queen and sole ruler of the king-dom; then she purged the messianic House of David and Solomon.

Help came from a single man, from Elijah, who grasped a new idea and experienced something new in humanity's history: the fruitful and beneficial effects of death for the life of the soul. He knew how nonsensical this experience would appear to his contemporaries and doubted whether enough people in Israel would live with the thought. The Lord comforted him with an inspiration on Mount Horeb-Sinai when, at the same time, he announced the fall of the old Israel: 'Yet I will leave seven thousand in Israel, all the knees that have not bowed to Baal, and every mouth that has not kissed him.' (1Kings 19:18). Elijah won for his people new spiritual leadership.

3.6 *Language and the archangel*

Language presents us with a force higher and stronger than that of the feelings; indeed, language itself con-tributes the most to the formation of the feeling element in the soul. After the Jewish poetess, Nelly Sachs, had lost her nation, the German folk, she lived in exile in Sweden. During the Second World War, she saw that the German nation was heading toward suicide, but there remained for her the comfort that 'language is homeland'.

After the collapse of traditional culture in the Third Reich, language appeared to offer the only remaining refuge. Yet after the Second World War, it became apparent that the population no longer loved its language. The universities introduced a mixture of Greek, Latin, French and English which deservedly went by the name of 'Volapük', 'world language'. They changed language into a naked vehicle for concepts.

The temptation came from English. The kind of language that only serves concepts was invented over two thousand years ago by the Roman, Cicero; this was a real accomplishment at that time. Cicero translated the Greek philosophical expressions, which were still relatively free and unfixed, into Latin in a fashion that strictly united word and concept. Cicero characterized every philosophical concept with one specific word. From then on, Latin had the tendency to connect every word with only one clearly outlined meaning. Old French preserved the virtue. Through the French-speaking Normans, the tendency was carried over to the Romance part of the English language. For this reason, a speaker of English usually uses Latin words in philosophy and science. On the other hand, the ten thousand one-syllable words inherited from Germanic and Saxon accurately characterize things and processes of nature, but are not easily raised to a level where they can serve as pictures for spiritual processes. When something intellectual is intended, Roman words are, of course, employed. English, however, leaves one helpless when the desire is to express anything in the realm of intellect and spirit which is new and does not fit into the old scheme of concepts; anything which can actually only be hinted at or indicated with a picture. English and the Romance languages are unable to convey imaginations in a simple fashion. They are outstanding languages of the earth; yet they are unsuited for the spirit that speaks in pictures (images), unsuited for heaven.

When the German universities adopted the English

approach to language after the Second World War, they denied the spirit of the German language. In his *Addresses to the German Nation* of 1807, Fichte discovered the unique power and possibility of the German language. It is able to elevate descriptions of things in the physical world to pictures for spiritual realities. For the rest of his life, Fichte devoted his work to studying the way that reason works with pictures. For seven years, his research consisted of almost nothing else. The angels think in pictures; the Bible shows this on almost every page, inescapably in the apocalyptic books. Fairy tales are also shadows of conversations between angels.

In the German language, everything can become a picture for something spiritual. The gesture of movement and action contained in words can become even more spiritual than the pictures taken from objects of the world. When properly employed, verbs can show relatively easily the essential nature of the spirits who work in our souls or create and heal our bodies.

Three thousand years ago in India, Sanskrit, the language of philosophy in Asia, displayed this wonderful ability. It was the richest language in the world in terms of grammatical forms, and its vocabulary, which consisted at that time of perhaps 50 000 words, was similar to English, which is poor in grammatical forms. Despite this, grammarians in the fifth century BC could list only 900 existing and 600 commonly used one-syllable word roots, all of which depicted activities, to which the entire language could be traced. Though the reconstruction and calculations are not perfect, they nevertheless characterize with one ingenious stroke the fundamental nature of this language.

The roots of English and German words are also usually to be found in verbs. This phenomenon points to the fact that things tend to be the result of actions and that the forms of things are based, in the final analysis, on the gestures of beings, on specific modes of activity of creative beings. Just as the organs of our body form themselves through the functions that they perform, and keep themselves healthy only by continuing to perform their functions, so too are the forms appearing in nature actually frozen gestures that have come forth from movements.

Because Sanskrit and German reveal this with every word and sentence, Fichte calls them 'primal languages'. Greek is a similar kind of language. Later, we shall say more concerning such relationships when we discuss the effects of the work of the spirits of form (exousiai) and the spirits of movement.

The Jewish wisdom tradition known as the cabbala considers Hebrew to be the primal language of mankind because the world of numbers is mirrored in its sounds. This world of numbers stands as law-giver to the active beings of heaven behind the tapestry of the sense-perceptible world. The interaction between the numbers concealed in the letters of the entire Old Testament is indeed astonishing. In addition, the consciousness of the sounds joined together with the numbers allows us to suspect that an even deeper spirituality can be reflected in the Hebrew language. For this reason, we can certainly count Hebrew among the primal languages in the sense intended by Fichte. Languages transparent for the spirit, such as German, Sanskrit, Greek and Hebrew, stand in contrast to the solid, hearty languages of the earth such as English, French and Latin. But German is the youngest and freshest of those fit for heaven. For this reason, it is also the most suitable for religious ritual at the present time.

Should the time ever come in Germany when there is almost no one remaining who loves the German language, there would still remain the hope that the unusual and powerful archangel of this language might recognize and accept those men who cultivate lofty rituals in German as his 'seven thousand', just as Elijah heard about the 'seven thousand' while on Mount Horeb. One would further hope that, despite all the denial, the spirit of the language would remain prepared to work further for the salvation of many human souls on earth.

3.7 *Language and the dead*

According to Rudolf Steiner, language accompanies for a long time the soul of one who has died. In so doing, it is spiritualized in the very same way that we characterized the possibilities inherent in German and Sanskrit as compared with the concrete, concept-targeted earth languages. The things of the earth and the words for them soon fall away from the departed. Words of action and movement remain; for such exist even in the realm of the soul.

For the first three days after death, the soul is occupied with the tableau of his life, in pictures. After this great vision has faded away, we hold the Funeral Service. In The Christian Community, the words for this ritual are framed in image, form and sound, so that they can remain in the memory of the deceased as the final impression from the earth and accompany him on his way. The words remaining with him longest are those of action; finally only the sounds of these words remain, but they are of colossal size and reflect whole worlds. When the departed reaches the stage of only remembering the sounds of the words, this is not an impoverishment for him — on the contrary, he now experiences worlds of spirit in the sounds. Then he finds himself already ascending into the realm of the archai.

3.8 The culture of an age

Above the archangels stand the archai. There is one arché to influence and leave its imprint on any kingdom that includes many peoples and languages. He not only extends his being over many countries, but above all, over long periods of time. For this reason, Steiner usually named the order of the 'beginnings' or principalities the *Zeitgeister,* spirits of time. They determine the essential character of manners and morals, and the stations of life with their occupations; they also exert a determining influence on the great communities of faith that stretch over many lands and centuries.

The Greek and Roman culture had a single unifying spirit of time and the Christian Middle Ages had another. Toward the end of the time of the Roman Caesars, between the years 410 (conquest of Rome by Alaric) and 565 (death of Justinian), the leading spirit of antiquity was separated from the peoples of the Mediterranean. At that time, there were a few great men such as Boethius, Cassiodorus and St Benedict, who understood how men could pray for a new *Zeitgeist,* a spirit to guide the age. In a few cloisters such men prepared the model of a new culture, the foundations for which they took from biblical Christianity. The noblest of Greek achievements still existing at that time they brought into the model: the seven liberal arts and the School of Athens thinking. In 529, the same year that Plato's Academy was closed in Athens by

Emperor Justinian, Benedict founded his cloister on Monte Cassino near Naples. The Rule of Benedict was later to be adopted for use in all western monasteries. Holy Scripture, the church fathers, and at least one great work by Plato, the *Timaeus,* all in Latin, were always diligently studied in the monasteries; and the youths recruited to continue the work of the monks were also instructed in these works, as hardly anyone else in the realm of the Latin church could read or write.

'Work and pray' was the motto which Benedict gave his community; and poverty, chastity and obedience were the vows of every monk. Soon there were no other places of culture than the monasteries. The basic rule declaring that every monk had to work with his hands combined with the three vows to transform the antiquitarian conception of life from the ground up; it was, so to speak, turned upside down. Even the Christian church fathers, following the older custom, did not have to do any physical work. A new culture was germinating in Benedict's monastery, which only encountered its inner limits after a thousand years during the Renaissance and Reformation. But even then, around the beginning of the sixteenth century, the need for a transformation of this culture was apparent, though its forces were in no way spent. Several denominations were created; the newest among them were started by Luther, Zwingli and Calvin. Each of these produced a branch of unsuspected strength a hundred years later.

In Calvinistic Holland, in Scotland and also in England, the followers of Calvin, calling themselves Puritans, found a new way of life, a 'pure' Christian life. Because they were persecuted in England, they fled to New England, where they founded new community states; for them North America was indeed 'God's own country'. In two essays of 1906–07 titled *The Protestant Ethic*, Max Weber again uncovered their rules of life. In addition to the Bible, the sources most used by the Puritan preachers were the ascetic writings of medieval monasticism, in particular the writings of the great Franciscan, Bonaventura (1221–74).

What Benedict achieved with an elite group of men in a monastery as a very special accomplishment was now carried over into everyday life and strictly required of everyone. The first rule was: work hard; only hard work makes it possible for the common man to lead the 'pure life'. The second rule was: live modestly; take the goods of this world which are offered to you and administer them for God. He will ask you at the judgment what you have done with them. Therefore, do not relinquish this office — with its responsibility to increase, to bestow and to administer — to anyone, not to a church, not to a welfare organization: do it yourself. And so it continues: procreation is given to man that he may bring forth children; any further use leads to an impure life, which God hates. The words of Peter as he stood before the council in Jerusalem sum up the intentions of the Puritans: 'We must obey God rather than men.' (Acts 5:29). And they felt that God's commands were to be found clearly stated in Holy Scripture. The Puritans were Benedict's strictest disciples. At the same time, they were religious individualists, not so much in their teachings as in their will to be responsible before God.

The second young shoot from the old trunk thrived under Luther's cultivation. It was called Prussia and its rule was: work hard and independently of reward. Live modestly and be satisfied with what is given you. Maintain discipline in all things; cultivate the family, but duty comes first. Duty is owed to the state, which must be served wherever it assigns you. No one leaves his post. In such service, God realizes his will. Even the king is a servant of the state. In brief, 'He who swears allegiance to the Prussian flag has nothing more that belongs to him.' Here, too, Benedict's words shine through —work, poverty, chastity, obedience and even prayer still find their places. This pattern bases life not on the practical decisions of the individual, as found with the Puritans, but rather, entirely as Benedict would have had it, on obedience to the community; the individual authorities placed above one were seen as representatives of God. Prussia inherited its inner life from German orders of knights, who themselves had inherited it from orders of monks, who received it from the Benedictine order. Prussia was a legitimate descendant of those who worked and prayed at Monte Cassino and at the same time it was the twin brother of New England. Both were born at the same time and both died from the same poison in the nineteenth century; a step by step forgetting of their ideals in the face of increasing wealth. With Prussia, capital in the industrial Ruhr conquered the poor servants of the state in the east at the middle of the nineteenth century. The royal court preferred wealth to the poverty of its earlier servants and all the subjects followed. The cloak which Frederick the Great wore when he worked has been preserved; it is threadbare, not from age, but from use. Since about a hundred years ago, no one in our society can afford to be seen in such a ragged piece of clothing. This was to be the fate of all of Prussia's moral forces — not merely of its voluntary poverty. The ethical spirit of Prussia had died by the year 1879, when the spiritual event we have already discussed took place.

Today in the western world, we win elections most easily when the fundamentals of Benedict's culture, which were laid down 1500 years ago, are individually and exactly named and then condemned as instruments of deception and oppression. When the word 'prayer' is spoken, we smile and are embarrassed. Of course, we are in favor of a shortened work week and higher pay. We seek prosperity for the masses; we are against sexual oppression; and we become indignant when we hear a word as antihuman as 'obedience'. These are the issues a politician needs for success today; more than these would only confuse the voters. The spiritual magnitude of a great text, such as the Gospels or the Rule of St Benedict, is seen most clearly when the devil distorts it; then it suddenly displays a power like black magic. The white magic that worked within it in earlier times is much more easily overlooked.

Germans today are without an archangel to cultivate their lives of feeling. Their present relationship to the *Zeitgeist* appears to be the same as their relationship to the folk spirit. This has led to the ruin of many simple souls who are without any inner stability. Yet, above and beyond this, Europe and America have lost their supporting *Zeitgeist*. That is far worse; for now the cultural and political leaders of the western world have no common orientation. Adding to the general confusion is the fundamentally false opinion shared by almost all of mankind that the previous spirit of western culture was the spirit of Christianity. Fortunately, that was not the case. It was rather the case that the specific spirit who prepared the way for St Benedict wanted to serve the Christ. The spirit of Christianity, however, stands high above him and found in him only one possible form of expression. The fact that a few people do have

115

this insight does not, of course, prevent the formation of world opinion to the contrary, and in particular it does not prevent modern young people from saying that Christianity itself has died out with the last few remnants of the culture of the Middle Ages. People will act in accordance with this opinion and Christians will be dealt with accordingly. A new *Zeitgeist*, who could lead mankind further, must be asked for in prayer. The conditions under which this can happen must be sought on higher levels of the spirit.

Should nothing out of the ordinary happen in the field of spiritual endeavor in the present age, mankind will find itself in the following condition: very soon, civilization will achieve a perfect technology simultaneously with a remote-controlled emptiness in human souls. Most human beings in Europe and America are on their way to complete, if unconscious, bondage. Our freedom is only possible to the degree that we personally concern ourselves with the spiritual world or at least with spiritual questions. Many people in decisive positions of leadership in the world today are not far from the inner state of mind in which they will no longer be able to understand any creative spirit from Homer to Goethe. The cultural achievements of three thousand years and longer will be forgotten. Indeed, in most ministries of culture in the world today, there are powerful forces working in this direction.

Further, in the biography of individual human beings, only the bodily and intellectual forces of youth will be prized; the mental and spiritual development of old age will be given a marginal significance or ascribed to pure illusion. What would be even worse, the reality within the soul will shape itself according to this picture.

Today any further development of our culture, in

terms of awakening souls, depends on the impact of a new spiritual power. Our final theme and the goal of this book is to awaken a sense for this new power. For without the presence of this power, at least in some modest degree, the souls of men will wither in the second half of their lives.

It would appear that thinkers such as Karl Jaspers have also arrived at this conclusion, even without a teaching of the hierarchies. However, without the Pauline teaching concerning the hierarchies, as re-enlivened by Rudolf Steiner, it is unlikely that anyone would have discovered an indication of the way out of the crisis in which our culture now finds itself. This 'way out' involved an insight by Rudolf Steiner concerning the work of the spirits of movement (dynameis). Today the spirits of movement are sending their forces to unite with those of the spirits of form (exousiai) in human thinking. Our attention must be directed to these two orders of angels today in a new way.

3.9 Powers of knowledge

The exousiai, or revealers, create for man not only his physical form, but also his clear thoughts. The form of the human body is perfected around the age of twenty-one. Artists begin to create valid works of art when they come of age, and beginning at about eighteen, many souls attempt to take by storm the world of great thoughts.

At eighteen or nineteen years of age, feeling and thinking do not yet want to separate from one another. The soul glows with enthusiasm when reading certain philosophical works: Fichte's *The Vocation of the Scholar* of 1794 is one such work. One could also name it *The Vocation of the (Thinking-Creating) Man*. The 1794 version is better by far than the lectures of the same title held in 1799. The young reader feels his consciousness awakened and clarified by Fichte's thinking; still, he would have a very difficult time if asked to repeat what he had just read. The time still ahead of him is for the development of precise memory and definite concepts. 'The hard work of the concept', as Hegel called it, is intended to begin only in the twenties.

Among those who lead mankind to thinking, Plato is the greatest, and therefore the high priest of the revealers on earth. With his greatest, most sublime thoughts, he appears to have even touched upon the realm of the kyriotetes, the spirits of wisdom. God, the highest which he thinks, reveals himself to Plato in much the same way as he is described in the Prologue to the Gospel of St John: as the One, the Good, as Being, Life and Thought (Logos). The cosmos of ideas only unfolds below him. There is a difference between viewing the heavenly throne in all its majesty at a distance and actually approaching the throne. In any case, Plato's philosophy did not extend to comprehend the dynamic metamorphoses, the changes that can occur in earthly existence. The dynameis or spirits of movement did not submit to his thinking soul.

The exousiai or the spirits of form still influence in a good way today the kind of thinking that is valid for all mankind. Their power alone, however, is no longer able to bring us as far as it could in the time of the Greeks and during the Middle Ages. Now they must unite with the dynameis in order to achieve as much. This uniting of forces must take place in human thinking itself. It involves a transformation in the activity of thinking, which is not at all easy. Feeling himself no longer supported by the exousiai, man today tends to retreat in the direction of the archai rather than to take on the additional exertion of raising himself to the dynameis. In that realm, however, he easily falls prey to evil beings, those who use traditional, emotional and closed systems of thought to imprint new dogmas into human souls. Men who are subject to these beings, then fight for the dogmas; for example, they conduct dubious social experiments with their fellow human beings for a century or so, perhaps only because they at least understand the theories behind them. They are unwilling to carry out the necessary thought work which would make such experiments superfluous. The door to evil lies in the voluntary restriction of thoughts where an expansion of thinking is both necessary and possible. One must even speak of a 'self-imposed immaturity' in man's thinking such as that ascribed by Kant to the Pre-Enlightenment Christians. Ironically enough, these same people consider themselves to be the executors of the will of the Enlightenment. This is true only by virtue of their feeble repetition of a few selected ideas new at that time; not because they unfolded any vigorous new powers of the human spirit and mind such as belonged to the Enlightenment.

For the thinkers of our age, everything remains to be done at this boundary within the life of mind and spirits; here questions, resignation, and sometimes — as with Nietzsche — even tragedy in thinking itself is unavoidable. Goethe began this work; in his theory of colors his intellectual discoveries were greatest, but the portrayal of his theory of metamorphosis is more readily accessible. What is needed now is a well-developed and carefully thought out theory of metamorphosis of the human personality, that is a philosophical doctrine of reincarnation. In this respect, Plato has supplied us more with pictures and myths than with supporting concepts. He felt the truth of reincarnation and thought *about* it, but did not really think his way *through* it.

Today, man's concern is to bring the power of the dynameis into the work of his inner life. In the final analysis, mankind's task will be to penetrate as far as the realm of the kyriotetes in this work. The path to that distant goal is a long one. First the dominions, or spirits of wisdom, will give us visions for enlightenment, which God himself will send into our souls. Only the dominions, according to Paul, are above all evil (Romans 8:38). *Kyrios Christos,* the Greek form of 'Christ the Lord', is the Domine, Lord, of the dominions or kyriotetes. Christ works particularly through this hierarchy, although his being ultimately stands above all the hierarchies as Paul says to the Philippians (2:10) and to the Colossians (1:16).

3.10 Six ascending moods

What I have not yet attained as a 'knower', I anticipate as a 'believer' — at least, to the extent that each new step in knowledge always confirms what had been believed. This is the role allotted to faith today. But our soul needs faith; it needs in picture form the goals toward which it must strive, which can only later be clearly and distinctly researched. As Paul said: 'for we walk by faith, not by sight' (2Cor.5:7); and later when he describes faith, hope and love as the powers of prayer, he says further: 'For now we see in a mirror dimly, but then face to face' (1Cor.13:12).

Faith in the existence of repeated earth lives, that is, in reincarnation, is a very effective motivation for moral action or at least for avoiding immoral behavior. Evidence for this can be found in India. However, only faith in the resurrection at the end of this material earth can give our existence its real meaning. It operates far beyond the common motivations of life; it provides an incentive for tireless work, in particular when it is combined with clear ideas concerning man's contribution to the future renewal of the earth on a higher plane. This faith can give man the incentive to work far into old age.

Through the proper attitude of devotion and reverence, we can now create the necessary preconditions in our soul for what we will only be able to master with our thinking in the far distant future. Plato also pointed this out; it is not the intellect alone which thinks, but rather the whole soul is engaged. Religion has no need to limp behind science, as it has so often done in recent centuries; it can reach ahead and anticipate new developments and thereby create the preconditions necessary for future knowledge and action.

Everyone knows the pain, the cold and hardness which arise when we ourselves doubt, criticize, or are forced to pass judgment on others. These feelings quietly arise in our hearts and accompany our other actions, thoughts and feelings. They sometimes become quite distinct. Yet every one of us also knows reverence, which is a positive feeling of an entirely different sort. In his *Theologia Platonis* (3:18; 151.50f) Proclus (AD 410–485), a late disciple of Plato, describes the sequence of feelings Penelope must go through before she can recognize her husband Odysseus with absolute certainty, after he has returned home aged and disguised as a beggar. Such feelings within the soul which create favorable conditions for knowledge are known as 'moods'. According to Plato and Proclus, the most fundamental of them all is *wonder*.

We shall now describe a possible sequence of such moods using the concept of the higher hierarchies from the exousiai upwards. Mankind would do well to cultivate these moods if it wants to advance beyond its present condition. The same holds true for the individual: if he would inwardly grow while outwardly aging. For if he achieves this, his later years can also become the greatest. The later works of Plato, Goethe and Steiner are the best examples of this.

Wonder, or a receptivity that respectfully acknowledges what is received without quick judgment, is the right mood to cultivate when we are faced with the works of the revealers or exousiai.

Developing flexibility in following the thoughts and spiritual paths of other people and no less in following the transformations of form in nature, is the effort which first allows us to raise ourselves to the dynameis. The thinker who would cast his net over the world and expect to pull in one prize after another is still working only in the realm of the exousiai. In the realm of the dynameis, the net must sink into the world of appearances and be lost to sight, so to speak. The fisherman can only wait to see if the sought-after fish voluntarily reveals its secrets. This cannot be accomplished easily and is achieved only by those who are not afraid to ask questions. Furthermore, he must have patience and renounce wishing.

In a fairy tale by the brothers Grimm, 'The Fisherman and his Wife', the fisherman, apologizing for his wife's greediness, says to the fish:

> 'Flounder, flounder in the sea,
> Come, I pray thee here to me;

> For my wife, good Ilsabil
> Wills not as I'd have her will.'

It was his wife's misfortune to harbor wishes and ever more wishes. On the other hand, a proper fisherman and a proper thinker altogether breaks the habit of wishing. Even curiosity is excluded. To discover anything else on this level other than what the world itself voluntarily supplies would no longer lead to truth, and would, when translated into action, bring misfortune.

Under the influence of the dynameis, no-one who thinks that the world should unfold according to the thoughts in his own head or who uses other people's disappointing actions to flatter himself can any longer live correctly; he will inevitably hinder the course of the world. In the company of the dynameis, only Jesus' way of praying is still valid. After something quite definite has been prayed for, there follow the words '. . . nevertheless, not as I will, but as thou wilt' (Matt.26:39). Resignation and devotion are the proper moods in the face of the spirits of movement.

The kyriotetes, with whom the true, the good and the life-awakening are one, helped Goethe to the words: 'Only that which is fruitful is true.' They themselves are entirely filled with wonder for the sacrifice of the thrones above them. Bestowing virtue is their life as it works downward through lower spheres. They stimulate life and, through their very looking at us, enkindle visions of the spirit and eternal life. Their glance does not rest on those who have reservations about imitation.

Jesus spoke out of this sphere when he spoke to the rich young man, who was already on the path of virtue and sought eternal life: 'And Jesus looking upon him loved him, and said to him, "You lack one thing; go,

123

sell what you have, and give to the poor, and you will have treasure in heaven; and come, follow me." ' (Mark 10:21.) For him who cannot feel wonder, all the glories on earth and in heaven remain closed.

The thrones are spirits of will, and are filled with the courage that creates a world in the face of nothingness. The power and the mood which we must find to stand before them lies in Fichte's thinking, which sensed that the eternal and conscious 'I' of man has, in the face of nothingness first of all to assert itself as self, and only then can enter into action and knowledge. This power lies even more deeply in the words of Jesus spoken to his enemies in the Temple at the Feast of Tabernacles: 'my teaching is not mine, but his who sent me; if any man's will is to do his will, he shall know whether the teaching is from God or whether I am speaking on my own authority.' (John 7:16f).

The cherubim order the widths and depths of the whole universe. We may very tentatively approach them when we inquire of and permit ourselves to be informed by a feeling which goes far beyond thinking and knowing to unite us with the whole world and which we call in such cases conscience, a feeling which warns us when we are about to touch areas where our shortcomings would only cause death and destruction. Cherubim are also the sentries before the gates of paradise, '. . . to guard the way to the tree of life' (Gen.3:24).

The moods of awe, resignation and unreserved wonder, devotion, courage, conscience and love are modes of behavior of the soul which are hidden. They are not forces of the head which would lead directly to knowledge; they are powers of the heart, which with patience prepare the way for profound insights and perhaps one day also for enlightenment. They are steps of a heavenly ladder such as the old patriarch dreamed of when he was in a difficult situation (Gen.28:12–17):

> And he dreamed that there was a ladder set up on the earth, and the top of it reached to heaven; and behold, the angels of God were ascending and descending on it! And behold, the LORD stood above it and said, '. . . Behold, I am with you and will keep you wherever you go . . .' Then Jacob awoke from his sleep and said, 'Surely the LORD is in this place; and I did not know it . . . How awesome is this place! This is none other than the house of God, and this is the gate of heaven.'

Adam Bittleston

Our Spiritual Companions

*From Angels and Archangels
to Cherubim and Seraphim*

During the last hundred years, many people have realized it is not only our conscious mind that matters, but that we are influenced by the far wider realm of the so-called unconscious. Many powers — helpers and tempters — work into this, and are well aware of what they are doing; as they are generally invisible to our eyes we may speak of them as spiritual powers. What then of human freedom? For a free action depends on an idea that we have developed consciously.

This book tells mainly of the helpful spiritual powers both in human life and in nature, who support and do not hinder human freedom. To know about their work can bring order into much that may have seemed chaotic and meaningless in life. The author draws both on ancient traditions which spoke of Angels and Archangels and of the great beings up to Cherubim and Seraphim and upon the revelation of the spirit which is breaking through in our time. Such studies can spread far beyond our own personal achievement of maturity.

Floris Books

Julian Sleigh

Thirteen to Nineteen
Growing Free

Adolescence creeps quietly into the life of a child bringing many changes and much inner conflict. The author sheds light on the familiar problems of loneliness, meeting others and relating to them, difficulties with parents, awakening of sexuality, drink and drugs.

Is adolescence just a burst of freedom lasting only a few tender and often chaotic and painful years, or can this freedom be preserved and grow in spite of the narrowing-down of options as adulthood approaches? This is the vital question each adolescent faces.

Without giving rules Julian Sleigh shows the young person awakening to make decisions out of his or her own sense of responsibility and feelings. If parents and adults are sufficiently aware of this time of trial and error they will be able to show trust and confidence in the emerging personality.

Floris Books

Michael Debus

The Search for Identity Conscience and Rebirth

Each of us at some time must ponder questions of our true identity and our responsibility towards life. Is the importance of life diminished if we do not die once and for all but go through death over and over again?

The author shows that a Christian understanding of rebirth or reincarnation demands that we begin to perceive its laws active in daily life. In learning to free ourselves from identification we can with our experience discover an evolving 'I' beyond our temporary states of consciousness, our sense impressions and our possessions. This 'I' makes itself known to us in the voice of conscience, leading to a new resolution, a new identification. In freedom it releases us and binds us again. So it is with reincarnation: conscience leads us into death and after death into the resolution to be reborn, with new abilities.

Floris Books